Soul Lessons and Soul Purpose

Also by Sonia Choquette

Books and Card Decks

The Answer Is Simple (available August 2008)
Ask Your Guides
Ask Your Guides Oracle Cards
Diary of a Psychic
Divine Guidance Oracle Cards (available October 2008)
Our Time Has Come (available April 2008)
Soul Lessons and Soul Purpose Oracle Cards
Trust Your Vibes
Trust Your Vibes at Work, and Let Them Work for You
Trust Your Vibes Oracle Cards
Vitamins for the Soul

CD Programs

Attunement to Higher Vibrational Living (4-CD set),
with Mark Stanton Welch
How to Trust Your Vibes at Work and Let Them Work for You
(4-CD set)
Trust Your Vibes (6-CD set)

All of the above are available at your
local bookstore, or may be ordered by visiting:

Hay House USA: **www.hayhouse.com**®
Hay House Australia: **www.hayhouse.com.au**
Hay House UK: **www.hayhouse.co.uk**
Hay House South Africa: **orders@psdprom.co.za**
Hay House India: **www.hayhouseindia.co.in**

Soul Lessons and Soul Purpose

A Channeled Guide to Why You Are Here

Sonia Choquette

HAY HOUSE, INC.
Carlsbad, California
London • Sydney • Johannesburg
Vancouver • Hong Kong • New Delhi

Published and distributed in the United States by: Hay House, Inc.: www.hayhouse.
com • *Published and distributed in Australia by:* Hay House Australia Pty. Ltd.: www.
hayhouse.com.au • *Published and distributed in the United Kingdom by:* Hay House
UK, Ltd.: www.hayhouse.co.uk • *Published and distributed in the Republic of South
Africa by:* Hay House SA (Pty), Ltd.: orders@psdprom.co.za • *Distributed in Canada
by:* Raincoast: www.raincoast.com • *Published in India by:* Hay House Publishers India:
www.hayhouseindia.co.in

Editorial supervision: Jill Kramer • *Design:* Tricia Breidenthal

Library of Congress Cataloging-in-Publication Data

Choquette, Sonia.
  Soul lessons and soul purpose : a channeled guide to why you are here / Sonia
Choquette.
    p. cm.
  ISBN-13: 978-1-4019-0788-4 (hardcover)
  ISBN-13: 978-1-4019-0789-1 (tradepaper) 1. Parapsychology. 2. Spiritual life--
Miscellanea. I. Title.
  BF1031.C523 2007
  133.9--dc22   2006024671

Hardcover ISBN: 978-1-4019-0788-4
Tradepaper ISBN: 978-1-4019-0789-1

10 09 08 07   4 3 2 1
1st edition, May 2007

Printed in the United States of America

 I want to dedicate this book
to all my loving guides,
on this plane and in spirit,
especially Joachim, Elephelia, and
the Emissaries of the Third Ray.

Contents

Preface

Last January I was invited to teach for a week on a beautiful cruise ship sailing along the western coast of Mexico. One warm evening after a delicious dinner, I decided, before returning to my cabin, that I'd go to the upper deck and meditate under the starry sky. Quietly expressing my gratitude for being given such a blessed opportunity to share my gifts, I asked the Universe for guidance and direction about my purpose in life—that is, the next best step to take in my work and service to others at this time.

Quite clearly, and out of the blue, I was immediately instructed by a group of light beings called the *Emissaries of the Third Ray*, whose primary spokesperson is a guide who calls himself *Joachim*, and who have been communicating with me for more than two years now, to channel a book titled *Soul Lessons and Soul Purpose*. Taken aback by such specific direction and already committed to writing another book, I asked the Emissaries if it was something that could wait . . . at least until I finished the project I was working on.

Neither agreeing nor disagreeing, they simply restated that I was to channel a book called *Soul Lessons and Soul Purpose*, in which they would provide direct instruction on how to fulfill our Purpose on Earth. And I was to begin soon.

I shared the news with my publisher, Reid Tracy, the next day, and his response was, "If that's what you are guided to do, then let's do it!" And so we agreed.

After the cruise ended, I raced home to finish the project I'd been working on, although it took me several more months to complete, all the while ever mindful of my guides waiting patiently on the sidelines for me to complete the task and begin this new assignment.

The fact that I was unable to begin writing immediately didn't deter the Emissaries at all. They ignored what I was doing and began downloading more information to me regarding what I was to write. They showed me exactly how they wanted the book organized. It was to be laid out in a very clear format of 22 lessons, which they said I'd understand. Intuitively, this number did make sense to me. For one thing, a great deal of my past esoteric training and metaphysical education was based on numerology, which is the study of the mathematical order of the Universe. In this system, 22 is a sacred number that reflects how the physical world is manifested. And in my studies of western Kabbalah, this number is considered the foundation of all things.

I also know from my personal studies over the past—yes, 22 years—that the first 22 numbers symbolize the cosmic principles behind all manifestation. In addition to the spiritual importance of the first 22 numbers, the Hebrew alphabet is composed of 22 letters, each corresponding to a number that represents certain spiritual laws.

There are also 22 archetypes found in the Major Arcana of the Tarot deck, a large and significant part of my education and background. In every one of my spiritual traditions, 22 is an important and even sacred number, so being guided to lay this book out in 22 simple lessons made perfect sense to me.

I was also led to organize the chapters in a certain way, each building on the next. I was not to insist that readers necessarily follow the given order, but was told to encourage them to let their inner guidance be the instructor and to work in their own way. I was merely to channel the curriculum; the reader's inner voice was to guide its assimilation.

Most of all, the Emissaries told me that I've been preparing to bring this information forward for many years—even lifetimes—and the moment was now. Being the messenger to share this information was part of my purpose, and it was time to fulfill it. My guides said I was to simply allow them to write through me, and that they'd do the work. I'd never been instructed to channel a book before, so I was excited about the experience.

Because of the Emissaries' influence, their distinct voice comes through in these pages. It's strong, clear, and no-nonsense. The guides speak to the highest level of our consciousness, the most awake part of us. They've been known to be quite frank at times, and their advice is unsentimental, but always unconditionally loving. They quickly cut through ego resistance and speak to our authentic selves.

As such, as you read, you'll sense their vibration, feel their presence, and know that they have confidence in you.

My guides have made it very clear that the time for us to learn these soul lessons, open our hearts, and raise our vibration on the Earth plane is *now*. We can no longer remain leisurely unconscious, irresponsible to ourselves and others, and tethered to ignorance and ego without suffering great losses. The Earth changes such as tsunamis, massive earthquakes, and epic hurricanes that are presently being unleashed are in direct response to our resistance to higher vibration and our refusal to grow, awaken our souls, and open our hearts. The upsets will worsen if our energy doesn't shift and elevate to a higher, more loving level. The sooner we individually raise our vibrations, the sooner we'll collectively heal the suffering on the planet. We have no time to waste.

I was instructed that this book is to be a simple, direct manual. It lays each soul lesson out step-by-step so that anyone—whether a novice or a master—willing to raise their personal vibration and assume their true Divine nature can follow along. The parts in regular print have been dictated to me by the guides. The portions written in italics are my own contributions and stories and are not channeled. I hope that in these pages, we'll all gain clarity and direction on our respective paths.

My highest purpose, in addition to serving as an intuitive guide and messenger, has always been as a teacher of spiritual law. It's my greatest joy to serve as a conduit between the Emissaries of the Third Ray and you in sharing these lessons. I trust that they'll open the way to your creative fulfillment and peace of mind. I hope that they offer a key to the door leading to your true Divine Nature. So let's begin.

Introduction

by The Emissaries of the Third Ray

W elcome. This book contains instruction for you to become masters of your human experience and to live as unlimited spiritual beings, free from negative patterns that tether you to your ego and suffering. We are here to help you fulfill your purpose on Earth, which is to evolve from an ego-bound, mortal, limited being to a spirit-embodied, immortal, Divine, unlimited being. Earth is your classroom. It is the only place in the Universe where you can physically experience your creations directly. It is the laboratory for your learning and experimenting, and the incubator for your greatness. The highest contribution you can make to this planet is to become the master of love and light that you are designed by the Great Creator to be.

This is a guide on how to quickly evolve into a light-embodied being. It shows you the direct path to higher vibrational living in 22 steps, while offering ways to measure your progress and know that you are advancing.

You will be drawn to this book if you are ready to undertake your true purpose on Earth. It speaks to those who have no resistance to becoming masters of their lives. As you read these pages, do not allow yourself to get intimidated or overwhelmed by the content. There is a lot of information and direction to absorb and integrate into your being, but you have tremendous amounts of spiritual aid to help you succeed, including ours. Although you are here to master Divine Expression, you are not alone in your efforts. The minute you decide to begin your soul's purpose, your angels and guides, light beings such as us, and your Higher Self will immediately step in to assist you. If your heart is open, you will receive loving guidance every step of the way—beyond anything your mortal ego can imagine. The benevolent forces of the Universe want to support you.

As you work, it is important not to perceive your life on Earth as reform school or a place to escape from, as many spiritually oriented students do. Rather, think of it as *opportunity* school. The Earth plane is the only energetic place in the Universe where you get direct feedback about every choice you make, showing you whether or not you are on the right track. Because you are immortal, you return to Earth again and again until you learn. As a result, no one fails to fulfill their purpose, and no one gets left behind. In the end, all souls evolve.

Eventually you will all learn your soul lessons, one way or another. The distressing news is that you humans, as a collective race, are not doing well in your curriculum at this time. This is reflected in the deteriorating conditions on the Earth plane—both in the environment and in your relationships with one another. This failure to love and express light is felt throughout the Universe.

As beings from a higher realm, we are streaming down in waves of light to assist you in rising out of these confusing states. As Divine tutors, we are activating the collective memory of your sacred heritage and helping you get back on track with your soul lessons and higher purpose. With this infusion of transcendent guidance, more and more people's hearts are being opened. An increasing number of individuals are returning to clarity and remembering their true purpose on Earth: to become living expressions of Divinity.

All humans are in this classroom together, serving one another as both teachers and students. When one person flounders, you can look to others for guidance. Like individual cells in one spirit body, each of you contributes your personal growth to the health of humanity as a whole. No one is dispensable. Like every cell, every soul matters.

Although you are united, you are not the same. Just as a body has many organs, tissues, and cells that make up the whole, each individual helps create the whole of humanity. And just as a break-down in one part of the body causes problems in other areas, so too does one person's arrested soul development hinder the entire race. On the other hand, when one aspect of the body is vibrant and alive, it restores, rejuvenates, and regenerates the other parts, returning health to the system.

Your personal vibration rises as you master your soul lessons; and it rejuvenates, restores, and reenergizes everyone you come into contact with. With every advance you make, you help heal this planet. You contribute to the earthly balance and furnish solutions to the problems of others. You serve in the highest way when you embrace your Spiritual Nature by modeling human possibility to others.

We in the Light realms have been called to serve you. We support your efforts, understand your frustrations, and champion your success, for your growth is essential to fulfilling the Divine plan. Your joy is everyone's joy, and your success is everyone's success—as well as God's. Until you reclaim your sacred self, the entire Universe suffers. Fulfilling your purpose helps everyone and everything. In turn, everyone else's efforts assist you.

In the process of soul mastery, everything in the Universe is ultimately moving toward the same goal of serving the Lord of Life through love and good works. We support you as your growth contributes to us, God, and the Divine plan. Enjoy reclaiming your holy nature, and be aware that you are assisted from the heavens. Ask for help, and be open to receiving it.

It is our greatest joy and honor to serve you. As a Divine child of the great Creator, you have access to all the aid and guidance that you need. You do not have to earn it; just allow it.

Your personal assignment is to live in peace and joy. Your purpose is to serve and love God within everything. Our light and love is with you.

How to Use This Book

The path to Soul Mastery is outlined in the following 22 soul lessons. Each one, if learned and fully integrated into your life, lays the groundwork and foundation for understanding and assimilating the next. They address consciousness on all levels—body, mind, emotions, and spirit—and serve to align your awareness solely with your Higher Self and true purpose.

The lessons are broken down into two levels: The first 11 are oriented mainly toward dismantling false ideals and breaking free from the ego, while the second 11 focus on elevating your awareness and vibration to fully unite with your Higher Self and Divine expression on Earth.

To fully embody each lesson, every soul must pass through four stages of learning: **student, apprentice, journeyman,** and **master.** If you are a student, the information will be completely new and offer a perspective that is different from your current way of thinking, perceiving, and living in the world. You can discern whether or not you are a student in a given lesson by looking at the degree to which you experience trouble or problems in your life with respect to that topic. The more frustration or suffering you have, the clearer the indication that you are a student.

If you are an apprentice in a particular lesson, the assignment will not be entirely new. You will have been exposed to it before and be intellectually open to learning it. Perhaps you have even actively sought mentors and role models to help you more deeply understand the subject at some point. You can tell if you are an apprentice in a certain soul teaching if you talk about it often—and think about it even more. You struggle with it and try to get around it if you can. Most of all, although you are open (somewhat) to learning, you secretly hope that you do not have to do anything different. You understand that you must shift, yet resist doing anything concrete to change.

When entering the journeyman phase of a soul lesson, your resistance begins to subside. You embrace the information on a heart level and actually begin putting it into practice. This is the "learning by doing" stage. As opposed to apprenticeship, where you intellectually embrace a teaching but take no action, at this point you throw your heart into it and start acting on it to the best of your ability. An apprentice asks life, "Why are you doing this to me?" while a journeyman wonders, "Why am I doing this to myself?" You now commit to assimilating the lesson. You recognize that all difficulties are an indication of what you need to learn, and take full responsibility for doing so.

When you are a master of a soul lesson, you have so fully embraced and incorporated it into your life that it ceases to cause any problem whatsoever. You experience the benefits of having learned that subject in every area of your life. You feel empowered and confident. Upon mastering a lesson, you begin to fulfill your purpose in that sphere; and your attainment serves as a model of inspiration for those in the student, apprentice, and journeyman phases. In this way, you encourage, guide, and give hope to others.

The lessons are laid out sequentially, so the easiest way to learn them is to approach them in order. The first one lays the foundation for the second, which prepares you for the third one—and so forth. The better you embrace and integrate one chapter, the easier it is to learn and assimilate the next.

That said, human beings are rarely consistent, so it should come as no surprise that in reviewing these teachings, you discover that you've hopscotched through them over lifetimes—learning some, skipping others, and miserably failing in areas—and now have a hodgepodge of awareness to sift through. If that is the case (as we are sure it is), review the lessons you know and live by (it is always good to review), and work on those you have skimmed or bypassed.

To assist you in understanding where you are relative to each lesson, we have laid out examples of student, apprentice, journeyman, and masterful expression at the end of each chapter. These will help you recognize where you are on the learning curve in that particular topic and what you must do to advance.

Don't worry about your current level. People are all at different stages in the various lessons. You may be a master in one and a student in another. You are rarely at the top or bottom in all 22 simultaneously.

As you move along the learning curve, you invite those who have mastered something ahead of you to shine, and your efforts encourage those behind you to try harder. Every phase of learning serves a purpose for you and others. Your struggle brings the best out in them, and their work brings out the best in you.

The curriculum laid out in this book is a course in Divine Law. It governs all living consciousness in the Universe; and is rigorous, challenging, and strict in its expectations. The Laws are impersonal, but once you begin to work with them, you will reap the rewards immediately. Your experience is your own best teacher, for it will reveal whether you are learning or not. Your personal joy will reflect your degree of success.

Read over each lesson carefully—several times. Contemplate it for a day or two, and let the information settle into your consciousness and heart. Notice whether or not it makes sense to you, and allow yourself time to embrace it.

At the end of each chapter, we have asked Sonia to offer simple suggestions to help you advance along the path of learning. Each small step moves you quickly to a higher vibration. Therefore, the learning process is gentle and nonintimidating. At no point are you asked to grow beyond your capacity—we simply invite you to step out of your comfort zone and try something new. The journey does not have to be painful, and, in fact, this instruction is actually intended to relieve your distress and daily suffering.

The only thing to avoid is a refusal to learn, which is the ego's attempt to block your Divinity. If you succumb to your ego, you lower the vibration of your soul and of the whole of humanity. Rejecting growth harms Earth and all those on it because you are part of the collective spirit of the human race. Rest assured that on a soul level, your desire to develop your full loving potential is greater than your ego's personal resistance. You will, therefore, get nudged again and again by the Universe to surrender any resistance to your Divinity—until your ego gives way to growth, acceptance, and higher vibration.

Approach these soul lessons in a relaxed, open-minded, and openhearted way. They are challenging to master, but we assure you that they are not nearly as difficult to embrace as they are to ignore. Neglecting these teachings makes life's journey miserable and uncreative.

Do not fear soul lessons, for there is nothing to be afraid of. They will liberate you from frustration and pain—not add more. Nor will they restrict your freedom. In fact, the opposite will occur: The more you embrace your spiritual nature, the more freedom you will gain.

The best way to approach these lessons is with curiosity and interest. As you will discover, you have already learned some of them, and you have even mastered others and are now expressing them as part of your purpose. In that regard, you will be delightfully surprised.

There is no need to master all 22 lessons in this life because the soul travels from one lifetime to the next with all past learning intact. Consciously or unconsciously, you have been working on these subjects for many incarnations, and you *are* progressing. Each sojourn on Earth serves as a classroom as you move up the learning curve. You come to all soul lessons at the perfect time, and no learning is ever lost.

Although completely skipping lessons is not allowed, you have all the time in the Universe to learn, as your gift from your Great Creator is free will. You can choose to progress quickly or slowly. The Earth plane and human experience is a soul school, and no one graduates without mastering all 22 lessons.

Approach these teachings with an open mind. Take satisfaction and pride in those that you have mastered, and persevere with the ones that present a challenge. Be diligent with your efforts until you succeed. Ask for help, and remember that as Divine Beings, nothing limits you except your thoughts. This instruction is intended to guide you, step-by-step, toward breaking free from patterns and behaviors that block your Divinity.

The fulfillment of your soul's highest purpose comes when you have mastered all 22 lessons and fully integrated your Higher Self as your true identity. At that time, you will be solely aligned with Divine consciousness in every moment of your life. You will fall into a blissful state, free of limitation and suffering. Your inner light will expand out into the world and beyond, bringing healing and harmony to all. In humble service to the Loving Lord of the Universe, who calls your light forward at this time, we recognize your Divinity and are honored to serve your evolution.

In peace and with great love,
The Emissaries of the Third Ray

PART 1

Learning to Use Your Creative Power

You Are a Divine Immortal Being

You are a Divine Immortal Being—a precious child of the Universe. Your primary purpose on Earth is to recognize your true nature as a Spiritual Creative Being. However, your ego, which is connected to your physical mortality, fights this truth in every way possible in order to maintain control of you, making you forget your real identity and throwing you into confusion and despair.

When you recognize that you are a Divine Immortal Being with the power to create and master many abilities, then trouble and despair subside; and your human experience becomes joyful, calm, and peaceful. If you do not recognize your Divinity and instead allow your ego to define you, you remain fearful, unhappy, and cut off from your true purpose on Earth—and unable to express your creative spirit.

As a Divine Immortal Being, the most important aspect of your purpose is to claim and master your creativity. The Earth plane and the human experience offer your soul the best possible classroom in which to discover this, learn though trial and error, and advance in every way. The ancient mystics of your realm referred to this process as *alchemy*, the process of turning the lead of your ego into the gold of your spirit.

You may wonder, *What exactly does being a Divine Immortal Being mean?* It signifies that you are not your body, personality, or ego; nor are you your past or future. You must not define yourself by experiences or conditions, for while these are tools you can use, they are not who you are.

You are *spirit*—a fiery, heavenly Intelligence created by God and unlimited in nature. You do not need to become "spiritual," as though there were something fundamentally flawed in you that you must correct or overcome, as so many of you believe. You *are* spirit. Embrace, express, love, and enjoy this.

There is no outside world from which you must gain acceptance or approval. There is only one human family, in which all people are intrinsically connected as a single Divine body. You are part of this community as well as a holy expression of love and a child of God.

The only thing blocking you from this awareness is your ego, which is part of your temporary physical vehicle—the body in which you learn while here on Earth. It tries to control everything and wants you to believe that it is in charge. The ego is fearful, manipulative, and confusing; and it will do everything in its power to distract you from knowing your spirit, your true self. Do not fall under its spell.

We do not recommend, however, trying to get rid of your ego, because in truth you cannot. As long as you are alive, so is it. Attempting to eradicate it is a wasteful cat-and-mouse game that will keep you from living in your spirit.

Instead, love and accept this troublesome aspect of yourself for what it is: the finite part of you wanting to be in control. Laugh at your ego (affectionately, of course), and ignore its perceptions. It is not the voice of your essential self, and it does not convey the truth. When you listen to your ego, you become consumed with negativity and fear. It will disturb your spirit with its endless insecurities, demands, and threats, which only grow if you pay attention to it for any length of time.

Rather than focusing on this false counsel, become attuned to your Divine Immortal Spirit. It will guide you to the truth that you are precious and that God, the Universe, your guides and angels, and we Emissaries adore you. As a blessed child of the spirit, you are made only of love. Learn to cherish yourself as God does—fully, freely, and unconditionally. You are here on Earth to accept and master this truth.

[As noted in the Preface, the portions of the book in regular print were dictated to me by the Emissaries of the Third Ray.

The sections written in italics are my own stories and reflections and are not channeled. —Sonia]

I remember the very first time I was introduced to this lesson. It came to me by way of my best friend and fellow psychic, Sue, when I was 11 years old. She brought it up while we were playing jacks at school. As I began my turn, Sue leaned over and whispered to me, "I have something to tell you."

Intrigued, I turned my head toward her but continued playing the game. She waited until I stopped so that she had my full attention, and then under her breath she said, "Guess what? We are God."

Shocked at her blasphemy, I sputtered, "What? Who? We, meaning you and me? How can you say that? It's—it's—wrong!" My reaction was instantaneous. Even though I was psychic and had strong personal connections with spirit beings, I was still a "good" Catholic girl—a straight-A student in religion, and I'd never ever heard such a narcissistic thing. I'd been told that we were sinners, born that way, and not even acceptable to heaven until we were baptized. Sue's suggesting that <u>we</u> were God was outrageous and antithetical to everything I'd been taught at school. It felt sacrilegious.

"Don't say that, especially out loud," I hushed her. "Sshhh!"

"No matter what you say," she responded calmly, "it's true."

Her quiet assurance was intriguing. How did she know? How could she be so bold, so fearless? After all, we were Catholic.

She waited until I'd calmed down, then quietly explained to me that she'd been doing some reading at the public library in the metaphysical section and had happened upon authors such as Ernest Holmes, Madame Blavatsky, and other theosophical teachers.

"In those books, great teachers say that we're Divine. I believe them, and you should, too," Sue said.

Her words scared me at the time. It seemed so . . . arrogant—at least according to my Catholic training. Yet on an intuitive, even organic, level, it resonated in my bones as true. It felt right, and I couldn't ignore that.

We stopped our discussion at that moment because I was afraid we'd be overheard and get in trouble. But her words planted a seed in me, and I couldn't dismiss the idea. I began to wonder about it, and I even sneaked to the library to read the metaphysical books she'd told me about. There it was—the same truth she'd shared.

By the time I was 14, the seeds of my personal Divinity had taken root. I didn't talk about it with others, except my mom, but she and my guides agreed with what Sue had said: We are Divine. Soon after, I was introduced to one of my most influential spiritual mentors, Dr. Tully. When I first heard him speak, he confirmed what Sue had suggested, and devoted an entire lecture to the sacred nature we all share. I believed him, and my purpose in life began.

Since then I've witnessed other people coming to this same basic soul awareness in many ways. It shocks some (as it did me), intrigues some, and scares others even more. But increasingly, this lesson mostly brings great relief. We are Divine beings, and the cells in our bodies know it. The sooner we accept it, the sooner we will all become more peaceful. We need to understand this now so that we'll stop acting from fear and rejecting ourselves and others out of a lack of self-love. We will all face a moment when this truth is presented to us. It's a secret that can no longer be kept from us. And when this awareness does emerge, it's our calling to this lesson, and it's time to begin our purpose.

Now you can apply this lesson.

— If you find that this is totally new information and that it is hard to believe there is anything Divine about you or anyone else, think it arrogant to have such grandiose thoughts, or have low self-esteem most of the time . . . then you are a **student** with respect to this teaching.

— If you recognize that you are a soul but hardly believe that you are holy; think it is possible to become Divine, but not in this lifetime; generally define yourself and the world by the opinions of others; and continually worry about your external appearance . . . then you are an **apprentice.**

— If you monitor your thoughts, think big, feel loved by God, and know that you are a Spiritual being . . . then you are in the **journeyman** phase.

— If you accept that you are Divine, have no resistance to your Immortal Spirit, experience a sacred life, or wonder how you can better create what you desire . . . then you are merrily on your way to **mastering** this lesson.

If You Are a **Student** . . .

- Take deep breaths and realize that they give you life. They are the foundation of your spirit.

- Wonder about your spirit and consider what "lights your fire" (so to speak) with joy.

- Pay attention to the similarities among people rather than their differences, and notice what is good—even great—about all human beings.

- Stop seeking approval from others, and accept your Divinity.

If You Are an **Apprentice** . . .

- Focus on the things that you love and appreciate about yourself, doing so out loud and often.

- Vocally give yourself full approval.

- Take the time to notice the activities that bring you peace and engage in them.

- Affirm that you are loved by your Creator.

If You Are a **Journeyman** . . .

- Remind yourself daily that you are Divine.

- Look into people's souls.

- Recognize the Spirit within all beings.

- Ignore any thought or feeling that makes you doubt your worthiness, and instead focus exclusively on living in Spirit.

If You Feel You Are on Your Way to **Mastering** this Lesson . . .

- Laugh at your ego, and enjoy your Spirit.

- Continue to model your self-love and acceptance.

- Be open to your Divine Nature.

- Love yourself without conditions.

Your Soul's Lesson
You Are a Divine Immortal Being

Your Soul's Purpose
To Love Yourself as God Loves You

You Are a Co-creator with the Divine

You are a co-creator with the Universe, and everything in your life is a direct reflection of how you are presently using your generative power. This includes your health, the quality of your relationships, your material status, the satisfaction or absence of it in your daily experiences, and your work.

It may overwhelm you to believe that you could possibly have that much influence. Nevertheless, it is true. You design all circumstances, but only rarely do you do so intentionally. You develop most situations unconsciously because you do not know how to use your creativity correctly to accomplish your true goals.

Do not confuse this lesson with blame, however. To reproach yourself would be like handing a child the keys to a car, watching him cause a ten-car pileup, and then suggesting that he intended to cause the crash. He may have provoked it, yes—but not on purpose.

As a Divine Being, you possess the ability to create on the Earth plane, but to successfully achieve what you truly desire, you must work within the framework of what is known as *Divine Law*. There are immutable principles ordained by God that govern how the physical world comes into existence. If you act in accordance with these holy precepts, you will attain anything you wish. Until you understand and accept that you are a co-creator and have chosen your life as it is today—albeit unconsciously, perhaps— you cannot master your soul lessons or fulfill your purpose.

The sooner you realize your innate creative power and learn how to use it properly, the sooner your life will become the joyful experience it is intended to be.

"You mean I created poverty, sickness, isolation, unemployment, social frustration, and struggle?" we hear you ask.

Actually, yes, you have . . . but again, not intentionally. You just learned from poor examples how to misuse rather than correctly direct your inherent Divine power. You basically have been doing what you've observed others doing—usually without questioning their behavior. For example, if your mother mishandled her creative energy regarding money and generated debt, then chances are you will do the same. It is likely that her parents also had problems in this area.

I spoke with a client named Rita several months ago over the phone. A self-proclaimed skeptic who had been encouraged to call me by her daughter, she told me right up front that she had a hard time believing anything, let alone what I might have to say.

Nonplussed as I scanned her energy and checked in with my guides, I asked her if her mother had just died of morbid obesity.

Shocked, Rita said that as a matter of fact, yes, that was true. Her mom had weighed 380 pounds at only 5'4" and had been heavy all of her life.

I then asked if she suffered from the same condition.

Rita was silent for a moment, then said, "I'd like to believe not, but I have to admit it's true. I'm also extremely overweight, but I'm taller than my mother, so I've convinced myself it's not as bad. I've never called myself morbidly obese, but I think my doctor would have no problem doing so."

I then asked if her daughter was also overweight, to which she blurted out, "Absolutely! More so than I am! I tell her it's a health hazard, but she says to mind my own business. It infuriates me, but looking at it from your point of view, I suppose she's right."

Rita then lapsed into a fit of despair. "Oh Lord, some days I just want to give up," she said.

I waited a moment or two for her emotions to calm down, and then asked if her mom had ever said the same thing.

"Every day of her life," she answered with a tone of resentment.

"And your daughter?" I asked. "How about her? Does she ever say she wants to stop trying?"

"Now that you mention it, yes, she does—all the time," Rita answered. "It enrages me when she's so negative."

"And you?" I continued. "Are you pessimistic?"

"I never thought myself to be, but I guess I have to say I am."

"And when you feel bad, you eat, right?"

"Of course I do. It softens the pain for a minute."

"From what my guides show me," I continued, "you and your daughter are simply creating the same pattern your mother modeled. Your weight issue is a thought pattern you've inherited and then passed along."

"All the women in my family are overweight," she said, and then laughed. "I guess we all learned the same thing."

"Yes, and here's the good news. Just as you've manifested this, you can produce something else as well—but not willfully, using your ego alone. You must co-create with the Universe in order to succeed. You have the power to generate unhappiness and misery—or health and joy. Just ask for help from your Divine assistant when designing your life, and things will improve."

Rita was silent for a minute or so, then took a breath and said, "I know you're right. I said I was skeptical, but the truth is that my own inner voice, or whatever you call it, had the same message. I just didn't want to hear, so I pretended I couldn't."

I suggested again that she consider her weight condition to be nothing more than an unconsciously adopted pattern that, with the aid of the Divine, could be changed. In her case, I recommended Overeaters Anonymous because it's an excellent training ground for using heavenly powers to create new circumstances, and it's free.

Rita must not have been nearly as resistant as she claimed. The next day she joined Overeaters Anonymous, and ten months later she wrote to say that she'd lost 60 pounds—and a lot of resentment. She stated that she was enjoying creating a new body and life for herself. The best part, she added, was that her daughter, Jolene, had just recently decided to change her thoughts as well, and they're now working together to develop a different legacy for themselves and future women in their family.

These misuses of creativity are no one's fault. They are just repetitive errors—patterns passed down from person to person, generation to generation, lifetime to lifetime. Your lesson is to stop these unconscious thought-forms from running your life and perpetuating problems, and to set new examples of imaginative power for others to follow, thus freeing them as well. That is why you are here—to consciously harness and direct your Divine energy rather than let it continue to run on autopilot, perpetuating the same mistakes.

At the moment, it is not necessary to concern yourself about how to better channel your creative power. Just accept that you have it, for you cannot master this gift before you claim ownership of it.

It may seem as though some areas of your life, such as the family you come from or the physical conditions and attributes you were born with, are beyond the realm of personal influence. But you are a timeless being who had past lives and a long history before you ever incarnated into your present form. So as far-fetched as this may sound to your ego, your soul *chose* your circumstances, including your family, body, and where you were born, in order to best serve your continuing evolution.

Each new lifetime carries on exactly where your previous one left off. This means that not only do you choose the setting of your present incarnation, but you also carry over attributes from your past lives as well. For example, if you were unproductive and overly dependent the last time you were on Earth, and did not learn how to redirect your creativity in order to become more self-supportive, you will continue to face conditions of lack in your subsequent appearances on the planet until you learn to manifest something different.

I have a client named Carlos who did accept his power and decided to make a radical change in his life with the assistance of the Divine. An engineer born in Mexico, he wanted to become a permanent U.S. resident and start a metaphysical healing center in El Paso, Texas, where he was working and living using a temporary visa.

Embracing his co-creative power, he applied for residency, only to be told by his attorney that he had a 50-50 chance of receiving it, and that even then, it would probably take several years for approval if he was lucky. Dismissing this prediction, Carlos asked the Universe to help him fulfill his intention; and seven months later, he received his residency card in the mail. His lawyer couldn't believe it, as the process normally requires several long and tedious steps, none of which they had even begun.

Continuing to co-create, rather than "figure it out" on his own or listen to others who discouraged him, he asked God to help him manifest a building for his healing center. Within a few short months, a structure that had just undergone more than $50,000 worth of renovations became available. Not only that, it had also recently been painted in the exact colors of Carlos's logo. He moved in and was able to set up shop within weeks—which everyone had said would be impossible.

"Left to my own devices," he said, "it's true that I would never have succeeded. But I'm a co-creator, and I asked the Universe to support my goals this time and work some magic for me. I wanted to do something different from what I was told I could do, or have seen others—and even myself—do in the past. I wanted to prove to everyone who said I couldn't achieve my dream that they were wrong."

Boy, did he! You can visit his healing center any time you are in El Paso. It's called <u>Butterflies of Wisdom</u>, and it's truly a transformational place.

You do not skip steps or have out-of-body epiphanies that allow you to bypass soul lessons. Instead, you move steadily along the learning curve, incrementally working toward fully assuming, expressing, and mastering your Divine Spirit on the physical plane. That is the joy of living in this world, and why your soul chooses to come to Earth. You can and *do* create all of the time. Once you learn how to do this in ways that please you, life becomes a limitless wonder of possibilities.

Now you can apply the lesson.

— If you do not believe that you can create anything now or that you have ever done so in the past, feel angry and helpless at the injustice of it all, think that you are being asked to be responsible for more than you can bear, or secretly hold out hope that sometime soon a prince or princess on a white horse will ride into your life to make it magically easier . . . then you are a **student** in this lesson.

— If you have been introduced to this idea before and find it intriguing or even fun to play around with, but don't take it too seriously; read self-help books (but don't finish them); or are encouraged but not convinced that you can make things better . . . then you are an **apprentice.**

— If you know you are a co-creator with the Universe, can't wait to improve your manifestation skills, pay close attention to your choices, or take full responsibility for the conditions in your life . . . then you are in the **journeyman** phase.

— If you wake up confident, focused, and ambitious about co-creating your next exciting goal; know with every cell in your body that you will succeed; approach life with optimistic ease coupled with steely and unwavering determination and discipline; and would never allow failure to enter your mind . . . then you have entered the **master's level** with regard to this teaching.

If You Are a **Student** . . .

- Make a list of all the present conditions in your life that you approve of and enjoy, take full credit for them.

- Make a list of all the circumstances that you are unhappy with; and observe whether other family members share them as part of a negative, learned pattern.

- Ponder the idea that you can create, and wonder what you would like to work on next.

- Read self-help books.

If You Are an **Apprentice** . . .

- Make a list of things that you want to accomplish now, and measure the amount of enthusiasm that each goal inspires in you.

- Only pursue those desires that greatly excite you. Forget the rest for now.

- Talk only about your successes. Be silent about your failures.

- Think of creating as playing with a magic wand. What possibilities would you like to develop right now?

If You Are a **Journeyman** . . .

- Every night before going to bed, jot down your day's creations.

- Make two columns: In column A, list successes and satisfying manifestations; in column B, describe bloopers.

- Next to the achievements in column A, note several things you did to bring them about. In column B, write down a few things you did or failed to do that caused disappointment.

- List those positive patterns that will lead to more happiness and accomplishment.

- Name the areas in which you are creatively strong and those with which you struggle.

- Look for negative habits that hinder your efforts to achieve your desires and that are absent with regard to your successes.

If You Are on Your Way to **Mastering** this Lesson . . .

- Celebrate your successes. Do not be shy, and do not downplay them. It is good and holy to honor your Divinity.

- Share your keys to fulfillment.

- Be supportive to students, apprentices, and journeyman, and help them when asked.

- Keep practicing, defining your dreams, and enjoying the process.

- Always remember to stay keenly focused.

Congratulations! You have overcome one of your greatest soul hurdles in accepting your Spiritual Nature and the power you have been given to co-create.

Your Soul's Lesson
You Are a Divine Co-creator

Your Soul's Purpose
In Fully Accepting Your Creative Power, You Honor and Respect Your Soul and Remind Others to Do the Same

CREATION BEGINS
WITH THOUGHT

A ll creation begins with thought. The process of manifestation is not random or haphazard, although it certainly can appear to be so to the uninformed or untrained eye. Rather, your imaginative power, and all such energy, follows Divine Law, which dictates that every development is initiated by the mind.

In your realm, quantum physicists confirm that everything in the Universe, including you and even us, is made of consciousness or thought. Ultimately, all aspects of existence, including your personal world, are essentially your musings, beliefs, and ideas made manifest.

Creating is a relatively simple process. If you choose good thoughts, beliefs, and ideas, you generate positive outcomes. Your lesson is to be deliberate in your thinking so that you produce desirable results. Examine how you have exercised your creativity so far by reflecting on your life as it is today. All that you observe has arisen from the way you use your mind.

Your thoughts create in one of two ways: either consciously in alignment with Divine Law; or unconsciously, carried away and manipulated by the chaos of the world. As you can imagine, the consequences of these two methods are vastly different. You act unconsciously when your attention is controlled by your ego and mesmerized by superficial phenomena. At this level, you are concentrating on negative self-images, insecurities, doubts, imagined disasters, exterior influences, past destructive patterns, and global fears—leading you to manifest sickness, stress, chaos, disappointment, and pain.

I have a client named Lynn who focuses her attention exclusively on being alone. An only child and orphan, she was abandoned by both her husband and then her boyfriend. She is so mesmerized by her solitude that she sabotages any effort by others to connect with her in a more intimate way. Although she desperately wants to create closeness and companionship, she dwells on loneliness. I've known her for ten years, and in that time, nothing has changed in her life. Until her mind-set shifts, nothing will.

Noticing where your attention rests can be a challenging task. Reflecting on my life, for example, I can easily see that I'm focused on my relationships with my daughters; working closely and intimately with my clients; creating positive connections with friends; and writing, teaching, and sharing my message with the world. Not surprisingly, those areas are flowing smoothly, and I'm quite happy with my manifestations.

To my shock, however, I've also noticed that I don't give enough attention to my husband, Patrick, and our relationship; to recreation and having fun (at least lately); and to relaxing (almost never). Needless to say, Patrick and I feel more distanced than ever. I'm also crankier than usual because I'm not playing much, and I'm chronically exhausted because I rarely stop.

Not satisfied with this, I've decided to look deeper. In doing so I've become aware of a buried layer of thought that has held my focus on a core level for a long time. I've been acting on the belief that I must constantly push and drive myself to serve God, and that my personal needs are far less noble to pursue. This is an attitude that I picked up in Catholic school 37 years ago (if not even earlier, in past lives), and it has been hanging on, creating an overextended, self-insensitive experience for me ever since.

I thought I was over that, and it actually surprises me that these mental habits still linger. What it shows me is how stubborn unconscious patterns can be. In fact, a huge part of our soul lesson is to bring to awareness what does hold our attention and examine it to see if it serves our spirit—and if not, change it. If our attention rests on positive, desirable creations, then we should leave it alone. But if it's held hostage by old, inherited misery, then we need to refocus in order to liberate ourselves.

You create consciously through intention, which selects your thoughts carefully and zeroes in on only those who serve a specific outcome. Having a clear objective directs your mind on an unwavering course and begins to bend and shape the physical world to match your desire. What appears resistant gives way to cooperation, and what was a struggle gives way to ease.

Intention dictates the course of creativity as it unfolds. The Universe submits to unyielding intention because it is the nature of Divine Law. Think of the various ways in which you have directed your thoughts, and note the results they have produced.

Recently, my older daughter, Sonia, got her first car and invited her younger sister, Sabrina, for an inaugural ride. Three blocks from our house, she hit a pothole in the road, which bent a tire rim and gave her a flat. She had the vehicle towed back to the dealership, where she explained what had happened. To her outrage, they said it was tough luck and not their problem, and told her that it would cost $350 to fix.

Wanting justice, she refused the verdict. Unwavering, she wrote the dealership manager, the automobile manufacturer, and the tire company, insisting that the damaged parts be immediately replaced without charge. She was so focused on the outcome she wanted that she wouldn't even entertain a conversation to the contrary.

Her desire prevailed. Not only did she receive a response less than 48 hours after her letters were received, she also was offered a new rim and tire as well as a year's worth of free car detailing and an apology from the manufacturer.

Was she surprised? No, she was resolute. This is a quick example of the power of intention. I never doubted she would succeed because I could tell how focused she was on her goal.

No thought is neutral or benign. All beliefs have power; and when you concentrate that force and direct it, whether consciously or unconsciously, it is bound to manifest something—without exception.

You do not have to monitor all of your thoughts to create desirable outcomes—just the ones that work against you. Some bring beautiful results, so leave them alone. Instead, pay attention to those ideas that are detrimental and undermine your life, and sort the productive ones from the counterproductive ones. Focus on the conditions and experiences you desire in your life. By virtue of Divine Law and the inherent power you possess as an Immortal Creative Being, these dreams will be fulfilled.

Now you can apply this lesson.

— If you are totally confused, have no idea what to focus on, are too worried to concentrate on anything, or place your attention on all that is wrong in the world . . . then you are a **student** in working with this lesson.

— If you agree that how you direct your mind *does* make somewhat of a difference in some areas of your life but not in all; practice positive thinking on occasion but mostly forget to do so; have a difficult time focusing on anything for a long period of time; or believe, and even fear, what you see on the news and television . . . then you are an **apprentice.**

— If you accept that your thoughts create, are attentive to them, notice where they serve you and where they do not, or are careful to think productively . . . then you are a **journeyman.**

— If you think creatively; review your beliefs regularly; focus on positive, happy thoughts most of the time; or are willing to leave no stone unturned to reveal unconscious, counterproductive, or negative mind patterns . . . then you are on your way to becoming a **master** of this teaching.

If You Are a **Student** . . .

- Notice the satisfying or positive results in your life, and appreciate that you created them.

- Observe where you place your attention, including what you think about, talk about, and hear others discuss.

- Turn off the television or radio, and hone in on your thoughts for a change.

- Create small successes, such as finding an ideal parking space or receiving a compliment at work.

- Work on becoming familiar with this creative power.

- Notice whether you have goals, or if you drift aimlessly from day to day.

- If you have no objectives, set a few small ones, and practice focusing on achieving them.

If You Are an **Apprentice** . . .

- Make a list of all your successful creations as far back as you can remember, and reflect on *how* you thought about them.

- Shift your attention away from what you do not like or want to what you *do* prefer and desire to experience.

- Talk, sing, write, think, and daydream about what you love, especially about yourself.

If You Are a **Journeyman** . . .

- Give your full attention to one thing that you love for an entire week.

- Write down what is not working in your life.

- Keep a journal of all your daily successes and how your thoughts, attention, and intentions played a role.

- Write down one intention for the week, and focus on it for 15 minutes every day.

If You Are on Your Way to **Mastering** this Lesson . . .

- When focusing on a desire, plan on a positive outcome.

- Start every morning with the intention to create an even better day than yesterday.

- Immediately recognize errant beliefs and say out loud: "Dis-Create."

- Think beautiful thoughts often.

Your Soul's Lesson
Thought Creates

Your Soul's Purpose
To Create Intentionally

Engage Your Feelings

To create you must also engage your feelings. Merely wanting something on an intellectual level is not enough to bring it about. Thoughts help organize this power, but unless they are propelled by emotion, they have no potency or drive. Desire, the most creative of all feelings, is the fiery energy of spirit that drives ideas into reality.

A dream is a gift from God. When you have a great yearning for something, your mind joins your heart and pushes for its fulfillment. Connecting mind to heart is essential for the creative force to be released. Reflect on those things in your life that bring you satisfaction. Are you able to identify the desire deep within you that brought these blessings to fruition?

I have a client named Jessica who has developed two movie scripts that have been sold and produced successfully. In both cases, not only did she resolve to write and sell an excellent screenplay, but her desire to enjoy the process and the outcome was all-consuming. When speaking to her about it, I could actually sense her heartfelt intention. She was on fire with creativity. At no point was she distracted by uncertainty about the future. She absolutely knew that her wishes would be fulfilled. So great was her conviction that every time I spoke with her, I knew it, too. The key to her achievement was that the project was driven by her heart, not her mind. She was passionate about her endeavor—so much so that she worked every day, becoming more enthusiastic all the time.

Her energy was intense, exciting, and contagious. The projects kept marching forward, step-by-step, gaining momentum and support along the way. The result was not one, but two feature films that were both imaginative and box-office hits. In other words, she succeeded with her intentions because she loved her creations, and her ardor attracted endless eagerness from others.

I had another client named Susan who was equally talented, if not arguably more so, and who also had a longing to produce a creative work—in this case, a play. The author of six acclaimed books of poetry, she shifted her focus and fixed her intention on playwriting. Complex and gifted with words, she wrote a play about Chicago and then set about getting it produced.

Watching her progress from the sidelines was a painful process. Clearly desirous of succeeding, but only somewhat focused on her intent, she limped along, gaining support here and there, depending on how she used her emotional energy. On the days when Susan felt clear and strong in her purpose and prepared to fully enjoy the steps along the way, the doors opened. She entered a playwriting contest and won; clearly, at that point, her head and heart were in complete unison. Buoyed by that triumph, she felt propelled to secure a theater to produce the play. This is the point where she lost her resolve and her intention wavered.

She hated the auditions and readings. People said they liked the play, but not enough to produce it. The project was dead in the water. After 10 or 15 rejections, she was devastated and focused her attention squarely on failing. She lost her passion and dwelled on the misery of rejection for five years. Finally, having had enough of that poor creation, she somehow rallied her enthusiasm, detached from her depression, and entered a national playwriting contest just for fun. Using her heart during the process rather than her fragile ego, she won. The prize was production of her play, and it ended up being produced in Chicago, then sent on to New York after earning critical acclaim.

After this, her first words to me were: "I don't know if my mind can take all of this."

It was a good statement. I suggested that she ask her heart instead, and she beamed. "In spite of the drama, this is very exciting, so sure, I'll keep on going," she said. And she has.

Your feeling nature—not your ego or intellect—drives the creative process. If you try to manifest something through sheer willpower rather than by trusting and following your desires, your mind goes 'round and 'round in circles as it tries to "figure things out," which only succeeds in causing anxiety and worry. The fire of imagination, which you need to move an idea forward into reality, comes from the heart.

I have a client named Tom, whom I've known for years, whose ego has continually undermined his success. He has long wanted to quit his teaching job, leave Chicago, and venture out west to live in the mountains, but when it comes to actually following his desire, he freezes. He's so uncomfortable and unwilling to let his heart initiate change, stemming from his fear of being the least bit out of control, that he becomes creatively paralyzed and implodes. His mind absolutely refuses to engage the furious energy of his heart, instead posing every question possible to stop him:

"What if this is a mistake?" "What if I can't find clients or a job?" "What if I give up everything I have and regret it later?" "What if it's lonely, difficult, and uncomfortable, or I'm disappointed?"

His attention is held hostage, his intention derails, and his heart is completely ignored. The result is a vicious cycle of continual frustration, worry, depression, and anxiety.

If you suffer from similar angst, it is because the essential head-to-heart, mind-to-soul connection is not established. Your ego is spinning out of control, while the heart sits dormant. Your mind is fruitlessly striving to provide the fuel you need to succeed, when, in fact, the required energy and desire can only come from your feeling nature. Attempting to create solely on an intellectual level is like trying to start a fire without a match.

This was the case for a client I read for named Sylvia. She and her husband, Derrick, sought to create major changes in their work experiences, yet both resisted letting their hearts participate. Sylvia believed that she ought to be a stay-at-home mom to her nine-year-old daughter because her mind said that it was the right thing to do. Never mind that she was bored at home and longed to do something creative like landscaping or flower arranging—even on just a part-time basis. She refused to follow her heart, explore her options, or trust that there might be a way to have it all.

Her husband, an attorney, also longed for something different. He wanted to work from home but wouldn't consider simplifying their expensive lifestyle. Instead, he let his ego and pride control his choices, resenting his job, his wife, and even his daughter. Both Derrick and Sylvia shut their hearts, fought endlessly over who should take care of whom, ignored their little girl because they were both so angry, and overspent to feel better.

The last I heard, they were living on credit cards—having to file for bankruptcy—and their marriage was hanging by a thread. Not one bit of their creative process involved their passionate feelings—they only used their controlling, furious minds.

As another example, my friend Erica is an incredible aesthetician who loves doing facials, microdermabrasion, and all the other kinds of cutting-edge, anti-aging processes. But she also wanted to work on her own, away from what she perceives as the toxic wasteland of plastic surgeons' offices. This was a tricky intention because the treatments she provides require equipment that must be purchased and supervised by a medical doctor.

Although disillusioned by the thought that her dream was impossible, she continued to press forward with her passion. Inch by inch and year by year, she persisted in taking courses to advance her skills, talking to everyone about her work desires, and building her reputation among the clients she had. One day, a doctor who'd heard about her incredible skills and demeanor called her. Not only did he agree to underwrite her equipment, he offered her a partnership and license that allowed her to be a part of his practice from her home. Amazing and highly unlikely, her success has exceeded her wildest dreams.

Imagine that your mind is like a car that can take you to the things you want. Your feelings are the fuel that fires it up and gets it moving. If you do not fully engage your emotions as the driving force behind your intentions, your creativity remains idle and dormant. Desire is the spark that sets the inventive impulse into action.

Now you can apply this lesson.

— If you are overwhelmed with fear, anxiety, and worry; tend to be sedentary; are unsure about what you desire; are overly analytical; and rarely tune in to your heart . . . then you are a **student** with regard to this lesson.

— If you agree that the heart matters but want to listen to it only if it is easy; worry some, but still fumble forward while trying to follow your yearnings; wish you could pay more attention to your heart but your brain keeps interrupting; or hear your feelings but you are not sure they are responsible enough . . . then you are an **apprentice.**

— If you consult your heart in all matters; get excited about things that speak to your emotions and creativity and are not afraid to show it; recognize that worry and anxiety means that you are thinking too much and therefore do physical exercise to stop this; believe in what you love and are involved in activities that you are enthusiastic about; follow your heart even if doing so is scary, uncomfortable, worrisome, or frightening—knowing that something good, true, and important will come out of all this drama; or choose a passionate life over a controlled one . . . then you are a **journeyman.**

— If you recognize that your heart is the voice of your spirit and engage it fully on every matter, enjoy your passions and make no effort to hide what you love, rarely worry, or are excited about your life now . . . then you are well on your way to **mastering** this lesson.

If You Are a **Student** . . .

- Wonder what might delight, surprise, and engage your heart.

- Loosen up and move more in order to think less. Walk, dance, bicycle, or exercise.

- Read children's stories, sing out loud, watch funny movies, go to the zoo, or get a pet (or play more with yours if you already have one).

- Reconnect with a childhood friend and reminisce about old times.

If You Are an **Apprentice** . . .

- Give people hearty handshakes, full eye contact, and heartfelt bear hugs when it is appropriate to do so.

- Talk about what you loved as a child, what you cherish now, and what you desire for the future, instead of focusing on problems.

- When worrying about things, thump your chest above your heart, let out the sound *Ha!* and then say, "Divine Spirit, clear this congestion."

- List all of your past creative attempts, whether successful or not, and remember how alive you felt pursuing them. Keep that feeling present in your awareness.

If You Are a **Journeyman** . . .

- Seek courageous and passionate companions to help rekindle your inner fire.

- Consider all past failed passions as good rough drafts, and laugh at them while admiring your spirit.

- Do something courageous, such as taking a trapeze class, trekking on a mountain, or volunteering to help someone who is sick or dying.

- Do something physical every day.

If You Are on Your Way to **Mastering** this Lesson . . .

- Let people know that you love your life.

- Listen to your heart and be very careful not to allow the outside world to override it.

- Do something once a week to fuel your passions. Eat a great meal. Go for a long bike ride. Watch an epic movie. See a musical. Throw a party.

Your Soul's Lesson
Feeling Is the Fuel of Creativity

Your Soul's Purpose
To Follow Your Heart

You Create in Pictures

O nce initiated through desire, the creative process moves forward in images. To manifest something, you must engage the subconscious mind, which does not respond to words. Its language is symbols and visual portrayals. Your saying "A picture is worth a thousand words" directly reveals the way to enlist the participation of this part of yourself.

Divine Law states that any image held constant will materialize. To grasp this concept, simply look at the physical world. The chair you are sitting in, the floor under your feet, the roof over your head, and even the clothes on your back came into existence as a result of a long-held vision being made manifest.

You can, for example, place all the best building materials in the world in front of an empty lot, but without a picture of how the house should come together, the woods and nails will lie dormant, and there will be no creation. The same holds true for everything you desire, whether it is a home, a job, a relationship, an adventure, or even a connection with God. Unless you hold a clear and consistent conception of your desired result in your mind, it will not materialize.

Without a precise vision, you get swept up in confusing, generic descriptions, which reflect the lowest common denominator of creativity and produce in your own life the drama, despair, and disappointment of the mass mind.

Not only must you have a clear image of what you intend to manifest, you must be able to hold that vision steady. Only then does the subconscious mind get the representation impressed upon it deeply enough to begin drawing that experience toward you. If you were to follow a blueprint to build a house, for example, yet found that every time you referred to it the plans had changed, you would become confused and lost and not succeed in your intention. You would fail to create what you wanted because you did not have a specific design in mind. You may try to substitute words or even feelings to compensate for your lack of clarity, but it does not work. If anything, it adds to the chaos.

If you recall our metaphor of thought as the vehicle of creativity and emotion as the fuel, you can also imagine vision as the destination. Without this mental picture, you may start your engine, but it will tend to idle, going nowhere or in circles. Or, like a car with no particular destination on the highway of life, you will get swept up in the daily crush of traffic, which pulls you in directions you do not want to go or leads you to become lost.

Some people are natural visionaries and do create in pictures. My mom was one of them. Every idea or desire she had was expressed on a sketch pad, whether it was a dress, a photography studio, a family trip, or even a party. The minute she "saw" something in her mind's eye, it would happen. That's how the basement and laundry room of our house became a beautiful studio and darkroom; remnant fabrics were transformed into handsome outfits for all seven of her children; and her hearing loss became an invitation to tune inward and listen to her Higher Self, angels, and guides. When she envisioned something, we saw it, too—and so did the world, because her inner sight literally pulled her ideas out of the ether and placed them squarely in front of her.

It is not uncommon to have a strong desire while, at the same time, holding a picture in your mind of just the opposite. Even though we want to create something new, we often get stuck on the image of what we have already developed in our lives and cannot move beyond it.

One client, a beautiful fashion designer, actually said after her third liposuction treatment, "I give up. Who am I kidding? I'm just a fat woman, no matter how thin I can temporarily become, and that's the truth."

Well, it wasn't "the truth." It was just her truth as created by her vision. Until she changes her mental pictures, her body will remain fat.

Seeing clearly and in detail shapes the physical world.

Perhaps the most exciting example of the power of creative imaging can be found in two small books called DreamHealer and DreamHealer 2 (available exclusively on Amazon.com). These volumes tell the story of how Adam, a teenage boy, uses his extraordinary power to heal the body. His vision is so lucid that he not only can see what he wants, he has the ability to actually look into the physical body and detect organs that aren't functioning properly. Using his gift, he envisions the afflicted organs and tissues as once again whole, and is so effective that his miraculous cures have been documented.

His most famous healing was of NASA astronaut and Institute of Noetic Sciences founder Edgar Mitchell, who suffered from pancreatic cancer. Working closely with Adam and doing visualizations according to Adam's instruction (along with the use of actual photos of a healthy pancreas), Mitchell reversed his cancer in four months, and it never returned again.

Adam isn't a spiritual guru or even particularly metaphysical. He's simply masterful at creating strong mental images, and consequently envisions people back to health.

Reflect again on your present life. Which areas are satisfying, and which are not? Do you see a correlation between the clarity of your vision and your level of success? Do you notice aspects in which your imaginings may be vague or contrary to your intention?

Sitting here writing this, I can't help but look at my own visioning skills. One of my creative desires is to be successful in my field, yet no matter how far I go in my work, I still don't feel quite accomplished enough. It occurs to me now that my blueprint for achievement is absolutely blank. It's a thought, an idea, even a feeling—and a true heartfelt desire—but I don't have a clear picture of what success looks like to me. So I'm aware that I've got some work to do on this lesson.

If your vision is vague, there is no creation. That is why so many people fail to manifest intentions such as prosperity, abundance, and even health. While the desire is there, the image is unclear. What is your mental picture of wealth? Of good fortune? You may have a desire for overflowing happiness yet hold a vision of prolific trouble. Do you see?

If you have struggled with meeting your basic financial needs, it may be difficult to envision prosperity. If this is your case, it would be more effective to imagine what you want such prosperity to deliver.

When Patrick and I were first married, we lived in an apartment without a dishwasher. Since Patrick was a sloppy cook, I spent hours and hours washing his dirty pots and pans as my part of the agreement for eating great food night after night. Several months into this arrangement, I began to question my role in the deal. He had the fun, and I had the mess. I wanted a portable dishwasher to help me out. Since we had very little disposable income, buying one was completely out of the question. The models we looked at were all over $500, which was way beyond our means. Still, I held the vision and kept my eye on the stores.

One day while visiting the appliance department at Sears once again, I saw my favorite portable dishwasher on sale as a floor model. Originally $589, it was now marked down to $250. Although it was still way out of our budget, I maintained the vision anyway.

Once home, I serendipitously ran into our landlord, whom I rarely saw. When he asked how I was, I suddenly found myself describing the portable dishwasher, how it was the perfect size for the apartment, and how it was on sale for 60 percent off. Then I asked if he minded paying for it. To my shock, and I'm sure his, he said yes. I had it in my home two hours later. Had I wasted my time visualizing money, I'm sure I would have never created the dishwasher for myself.

The more definite your vision, the more quickly you manifest the outcome. This holds true for material desires as well as emotional ones. The law works on all levels of human experience: mental, physical, and emotional—including love. This is perhaps one of the more challenging creations to envision, because your human experience of love is so confused, and in many cases this quality has been poorly modeled for you. You therefore do not hold a clear picture of what love is. If you have difficulty envisioning it, imagine what you seek to experience instead. For example, if you are lonely, see in your mind's eye a solid and generous companion with whom you spend quality and committed time, rather than trying to focus on the abstract concept of "love." If you want someone to share your life with, envision just that, including grocery shopping; eating; being sexually intimate; and walking, talking, and laughing together—whatever your picture of communal bliss is. A simple but clear vision is more powerful than a complicated but vague one, and will manifest much faster.

I had a client whose parents loved her very much but were controlling, angry people who menaced her with threats and yelling when she was a young child. It was no surprise to me that when she envisioned love, she met and married a domineering, hostile man much like her parents. She imagined what she had previously experienced. Soon divorced, she asked me how to succeed in future relationships. I suggested that she start by getting a clearer picture of self-love that included patience; a calm demeanor; affection; and peaceful, positive dialogue with her spirit.

She seemed confused. "I don't have any idea what that looks like," she said.

"That's your challenge and lesson," I responded. "Begin forming an idea, an image, or a clear vision, and the experience will follow."

It took her five years, through lots of trial and error, but eventually she succeeded.

"I pictured an adult who wasn't full of fear and who really enjoys me for who I am," she said. "I stayed clear in my vision, using my favorite high school teacher as my role model. I finally attracted exactly what I envisioned. And would you believe, he's a teacher!"

There is no limit to what you can create as long as you can visualize it. Do not concern yourself with how the desired creation will come about. The Universe will organize itself to produce the idea in your mind's eye. That is its part of the co-creation agreement. Your job is to hold the vision.

This is hard for the ego to believe and accept because it wants to be in the middle of the process, controlling everything. Even if this stubborn part of yourself is not involved, it throws up resistance to distract you. Remember, the ego does not make anything. Your spirit, your Immortal Divine self, is the creator. Smile at your ego, but do not allow it to interfere. Sharpen your visioning skills by studying clear examples of what you want to manifest. Watch others; look at movies, magazines, and even television; and read books that help you hone your mental imagery. Notice where your conceptualization is weak, and work to improve it.

Now you can apply these teachings.

— If you are unable to hold a clear vision of what you want; spend lots of time watching television (especially reality shows), reading newspapers, and fretting over what you have seen in this media; are cynical; see only the dark side, frustration, and obstacles to success; hold negative images, especially from the past; or spook yourself with scary or disappointing pictures of the present or future . . . then you are a **student** with regard to this lesson.

— If you occasionally try creative visualization and sometimes hold a positive vision, lust over other's people's happy life experiences, read about celebrities, watch *Entertainment Tonight,* wander through the nicer sections of stores, glance at beautiful magazines and imagine that one day the lives depicted in the pages could be yours, or fill your mind with visions of disaster but know that you are only scaring yourself . . . then you are an **apprentice.**

— If you hold a joyful, clear vision of what you want to create and experience; look for inspiring role models who are leading lives you dream of; use your free time to imagine exactly what you want in the most precise terms that you can determine; or are careful to feed your inner eye with specific, positive, and powerful images . . . then you are a **journeyman.**

— If you hold definite images to support your intentions, nourish yourself with a regular and steady stream of vivid, beautiful, and satisfying mental pictures; know that the minute you can see an experience clearly in your mind's eye and hold that image, you will attract it to you; or always envision the best . . . then you are on your way to **mastering** this lesson.

If You Are a **Student** . . .

• Notice what images you hold in your mind, speak about, and convey to others. Do they correspond to what you want or to what you do not desire?

• Become more proactive in defining the kinds of experiences you prefer and try to depict them visually. Make a collage, take photos, draw what you want to create, and look for examples in magazines.

• Stop acting as an unconscious trash receptacle for negative images, ideas, visions, and dreams.

• Focus on beauty instead of pain, destruction, and disappointment.

• Describe your vision to someone else. Keep going until they see it clearly.

If You Are an **Apprentice** . . .

• List the areas of frustration or disappointment in your life and notice the mental picture you hold around them.

• If you are maintaining a negative or counterproductive image, change it to one that aligns with what you actually want.

- Recognize how your ego tries to derail your vision through cynicism, distraction, and drama—and ignore these sabotaging tricks.

- Fill your mind with beautiful images by enjoying nature and visiting museums, galleries, showrooms, and shops filled with lovely, inspiring things. Study the look of your desired object, experience, or outcome until you are quite clear about what you intend.

If You Are a **Journeyman** . . .

- Spend 10 to 20 minutes a day envisioning your creative desire in your mind's eye.

- Scrutinize, discern, and discard negative images that hamper your progress by flushing them out with your awareness. Recognize that these visions are contrary to your intention.

- Make a collage of the things that you do not want in your life and display it. Let what you hold in your mind reflect back at you until you no longer wish to keep that image.

- Be mindful of the images that you convey to others. Controlling this is like running a movie projector—stop the movie, edit it, or change the reel when the pictures you share are not what you want to experience.

If You Are on Your Way to **Mastering** this Lesson . . .

- Take photos of your created successes and display them prominently in your home.

- Begin your morning, even before opening your eyes, by making a mental movie of what you intend for that day. Embellish, direct, and design your experience.

- Practice visioning specific things—such as phone calls, invitations, hugs and kisses—as creative exercises, seeing how many you can manifest in a day.

- Have fun every day imagining new creations that outdo the ones from the day before.

Your Soul's Lesson
Your Vision Creates Your Reality

Your Soul's Purpose
Envision Your Life Beautiful

Live in the Present

The power to create lies only in the present. You cannot manifest anything in the past or future, but only in the "now." When your focus is centered on this moment, you free up the energy you need to develop what you want. Your ego does not live in this way. Rather, it jumps back and forth from days long gone to those yet to come, losing all of its power to create in the instant. Dwelling on these other times steals your ability to create. The ego would have you believe that this protects you from negativity and disappointment, but this is a lie. It does not and *cannot* safeguard you in this manner because the power to do that, like the capacity to create, can only be found in the now. Your ego must be trained to be in the moment.

I'm reminded of how tricky (and challenging) it is to live in the here and now every single time I do an intuitive reading for a client. Not only do I observe the habits of people stuck in the past of this lifetime, I also see them reliving the patterns of former lives, as the soul carries the same bank of awareness from one incarnation to the next.

Just today, I had a dramatic reminder of this when doing a psychic reading for a woman over the phone. I saw that for many soul cycles she had been a slave girl, prostitute, or kept woman in a harem; and that for the most part, she had usually made her lives more comfortable by using her persuasive skills in flattering dominant male egos.

I could tell that her soul wanted to be released from all this negative dependency, to live in the now, and to confidently stand in her own power as a free and independent woman. Yet in spite of her desire, she found herself in the same situation in this life as in the past, trying to get an influential man to take care of her once again. Only this time her soul energy rebelled and wavered.

Sometimes she was aware of her strength in the now, such as when she focused on her selling and counseling abilities and felt good about her autonomy. Most of the time, however, she was preoccupied with re-creating old dependencies and ignored her present power. She obsessed about "being taken care of" and dreaded her future from fear that she wouldn't succeed in finding the "sugar daddy" she longed for.

"All you want," I said, smiling, "is to be completely supported by a man again, and you'll stop at nothing in your desire to return to the familiar."

She laughed so hard at this that I was surprised. I've heard people chuckle when their crazy patterns are exposed because it feels so liberating, but her reaction was over the top. When she regained composure, she said, "You don't know just how true that statement is. Every since I was a child, I've wanted to be a 'kept woman' supported by a rich man—except that I wasn't born female. I was born male—not gay, but simply a girl inside a boy's body. In fact, I just went through a four-year process to have a woman's body, but now that I do, I'm only mildly happier. I still can't seem to find the right man to take care of me, even though I'm gorgeous!"

Of course, this is an extreme example of someone getting stuck in the past. Regardless of what body her soul occupied, it wanted to live in the present; while her mind, emotions, and previous imprints held her back.

Living in the moment takes determination and discipline as the ego likes to replay—over and over—all slights and injustices, all routines (good or bad), and anything that is familiar in order to distract you from the present.

I had a client named Joan who was preoccupied not just with the past, but also the future; and this threw her life into absolute chaos and destruction. On the heels of being unceremoniously dumped by a womanizing boyfriend, she was suddenly pursued by a man who loved her very much.

Although still nursing her wounds, Joan nevertheless allowed herself to be wooed and ultimately (albeit reluctantly) married the new and far more caring man. Unwilling to give up her defenses, however, she continually dwelled on needing to keep her guard up, hold back, and protect herself "just in case," so that she wouldn't have to go through such humiliation again. Never mind that her current partner was kind, honest, open, and adoring. She was so stuck in the past and how she had been wronged—and so worried about the future and never letting herself get hurt again, that she ignored and dismissed her husband's love altogether. He tried for ten years to seduce her into living in the present and to open up, accept his love, and grow, but her focus didn't change. Joan's obsession with the past and her refusal to create a new life with him became too difficult for him to bear.

Not surprisingly, he met another woman at work who was willing to live in the moment with him. To Joan's shock, one day her husband left her and moved on. Not only had her preoccupation with other times kept her from enjoying the now, it actually re-created her experience of being dumped all over again.

Several years ago, a man named John showed up at my office because he was frustrated and stuck in his work. No matter what job he took, in less than six months he would invariably find his boss and peers unbearable and need to quit. Born with several large and unsightly birthmarks on his face, he'd been mercilessly taunted by the other kids at his all-boy's school, especially the older ones. Suffering from their cruel jibes, he became nearly suicidal.

When we was 30, he found a plastic surgeon who successfully removed the growths, and he emerged a very handsome man. Yet John remained stuck, still seeing himself as an "ugly" person. As a result, he stayed withdrawn, defensive, and suspicious, especially with other men. Not surprisingly, he isolated himself and alienated his co-workers in his male-dominated construction jobs. When he could no longer stand it, he'd quit. This pattern continued for 16 years. Caught up in a long-term vicious cycle born out of his past, he was usually broke and angry.

John had to undertake a serious review of his repeated ways of thinking and behaving to understand and realize that although he had *changed on the outside, he was mired in the past on the inside. With the help of a therapist, some major forgiveness work, and prayer, he finally arrived in the present. He decided to start his own construction company just to break his pattern. Last I heard, his business was doing quite well, and after three years, he's still sticking with it.*

When you place your attention fully in the present, you can also heal the past.

I observed the power of this focus in my own mother's life. As a child during World War II, she became lost during an evacuation in her home country of Romania and ended up, along with thousands of others, in a Nazi concentration camp in Germany. Liberated at the age of 15 and soon married to my father, an American soldier, she came to the United States to begin a new life. Like other young war brides, she got involved in numerous activities here, had many children, and rarely—if ever—talked about or reflected on the past. Doing so was too painful and produced no tangible good.

I still wanted to know more about her history in order to better understand her, so I talked my parents into returning to Germany with me for their 50th anniversary. When we arrived, I could see the anxiety, fear, and anguish of the past appear on her face. It grew more and more obvious during the first three days of our visit. On the fourth day, we went to a particularly painful site. As we approached, I could feel her heart thumping nearly out of her chest as I walked next to her. But as soon as we arrived at the gate, she suddenly noticed that despite the early winter frost, a group of small flowers was growing at the entrance.

She gasped at this sight, grabbed my father's hand, and said, "Look, Paul, there are flowers! Here!" Then, tears filling her eyes, she turned to me and exclaimed, "Nothing can stop life, Sonia. Nothing!" Squeezing my hand, she nodded and added, "This is a dream I don't want to revisit. There was no life for me then, so there's no need to go backward and re-create it now." Smiling, she went on, "Let's go and see what's new in town." And we left.

Who was I to argue? I knew that she was right. The present offered far more to her and to us than the past did. We shut that door together, went shopping, and had the best day of our lives.

Living in the moment does not only mean waking up from the past. It is also about not getting lost in thoughts about the future, believing that it holds some magical power that will ease your life. It is not that you should not expect or look forward to happy prospects. However, improving the quality of things to come is only possible when you live gloriously in the here and now.

The present, even with all its frustration and sorrow, is a gift from the Lord of the Universe. Every experience—pleasant or painful—deepens your soul and brings more learning to it.

Being very goal oriented, living in the moment rather than in the future is perhaps one of my greatest challenges. I love to plan, throw my awareness into possibilities, brainstorm, daydream, and believe that everything will keep improving and growing brighter.

But as I'm writing this, I'm acutely aware of—and slightly embarrassed by—how invested in the future I can be. It even makes me want to laugh at myself. Thoughts about what is to come keep me going 24 hours a day—even when I sleep. They also make me preoccupied, intense, and impatient, and take me away from the things I love, mainly my family.

I get way too caught up in trying to catch the future. On some days I almost feel that it's right at my fingertips, and I push myself faster and harder toward it. No wonder I get so worn out day after day. I simply can't ever reach this great tomorrow that I'm so busy creating.

It's interesting how my soul recently woke me up from this all-too-familiar mind game and brought me back to the now. My older daughter, Sonia, recently called me on her cell phone just as I was about to race out the door to work on "my future." Debating whether or not to even take the call, as I was headed to an important meeting, my spirit screamed, "Answer!"

The moment I said hello, I knew something was drastically wrong. Before Sonia said a word, dread flew through the phone line. Gasping, she screamed that her best friend had just been hit by a car right in front of her eyes. The young woman had been thrown over the length of the vehicle that had struck her and was lying on the side of the road. My daughter was waiting for the ambulance to arrive as we spoke. She was hysterical and traumatized beyond belief. Wracked by the impact and overwhelmed by the shock, she kept repeating, "It missed me by a centimeter. Oh, how could this happen so fast!"

That event snapped me back to the present immediately. Life stopped being a rushing river that I could barely manage, and instantly everything came to a frozen halt. My ego shut up. This was too intense to fight or even comment on.

Thankfully, this story has a happy ending. Sonia's friend, a gymnast, took the impact miraculously well, and didn't suffer more than a few minor scratches. She was back to her usual life in less than a week . . . and I was back to mine in less than a minute. The shock was a gift delivered to my soul. The possibility of losing my daughter or her friend reoriented my focus in seconds.

I was alive, and so were the two young women. It suddenly became crystal clear how much that mattered, and how my preoccupations had so effectively thrown me into a dead zone, where nothing lived.

I was so grateful to be back in the moment and met with so much grace that I completely shifted my awareness. I still have goals and create because I like it, but I definitely have resolved (for now) not to postpone any happiness and to live in the now instead. My focus is in the present—to heck with "the future." Now let's see if I can really learn the lesson this time!

The funny thing about this change is that ever since I made it, the things I kept pushing to create are now flying toward me, as though the more I stay in the moment, the more space there is in my life for the goodness I desire to expand naturally.

Do not remain arrested in unresolved childhood dramas. You are impacted by your family of origin because it is where you first learn your value, are introduced to relationships, and are given your earliest tools to navigate the world. But eventually you must recognize your family's limitations and the ways in which you feel that they have wounded you, forgive them, and move on.

Remember that your relatives are part of your soul school and that you have chosen them. They create an incubator or a hothouse, so to speak, where you can grow your soul as quickly as possible, and they actually serve you very well. However, your true parents are not here on this plane, but are the Divine Holy Father and Blessed Mother who created you. Your mom and dad are the sacred vessels who give you passage to Earth school, and are to be respected and honored for agreeing to do this, but they are not your true origin.

View your family as part of your soul's curriculum. This will give you perspective and compassion, and hopefully will motivate you to let go of any anger or grudges you have against them. Love these people, and realize that they are fumbling through Earth school just like you are. As long as you are here, you are all students, learning together and from one another. If you have realistic expectations of your family and everyone else, this will help you free yourself from the past and the future and begin to live in the moment.

Notice what is real and true in your life right now, even if it is painful. If you feel hurt, be aware of how acutely alive that feeling is. If you pay attention, you will see that most of your suffering is not centered in the present, but arises from a fear of possible future anguish that might be too much to bear.

This was the case for Michael. An ad executive by day, his creative soul was craving expression through music, writing, and poetry; and it wouldn't leave him alone. Although these arts were calling him, they frightened him, too. What if he quit his job to follow his spirit? What if in doing so he went broke? And what if this resulted in his wife getting angry and asking for a divorce? If she then took the kids—which would cause the worst suffering imaginable—it would leave him too shattered to create, and he could therefore end up homeless and alone on the street. What pain! What agony!

Scared by his own musings, he became overwhelmed and despondent, blamed his wife for his misery, and isolated himself from his children. He closed his musical heart and sulked around the house, having allowed his ego to flatten his creative soul.

Fortunately, I caught him in time. His family was about to leave because they were so shut out of his life. I convinced him to stop dwelling on the future and live in the present for a trial period of one month.

Desperately wanting to grow, he agreed. To support his intention, he wore a whistle around his neck and gave one to each family member as well, with instructions that every time he was caught living in the future, he'd hear a shrill blast.

It worked. It took three weeks to retrain his brain, but he got so tired of the whistles that he decided to really commit his focus to the present instead of merely "trying" to do so. The minute he made that choice, the doors to life's opportunities flew open for him. He began to write again and compose and play. He also started two bands, one with friends and one with his kids. The adult ensemble started performing in local clubs, and the children's group at birthday parties. Ask him about the future now, and he says, "I don't have time to think about it. But even so, it feels bright."

Remaining centered in present time takes practice. Notice what is in front of you now. Become aware of the colors, smells, lights, textures, landscapes, tastes, sounds, and energy. Pay attention to the fact that the more you stay in the moment, the more acutely your senses register your world. Feel the power and freedom that lies in this instant. When you are concentrating on the now, you have the opportunity and ability to choose and focus on what you desire.

Now you can apply this lesson.

— If you are obsessed with the past, continually worry about the future, get easily distracted so that you cannot concentrate on the moment, or are simply rarely aware of what is in front of you . . . then you are a **student** with regard to this lesson.

— If you want to live in the present but have unfinished business, family matters, or disappointments and betrayals from the past that just will not leave you alone; are willing to live in the now if you can only be sure that the future will be secure; have decided that *any* time frame is too much to think about and just want to zone out by meditating or using a mind altering drug, perhaps in order to be one with God; or are convinced that you have ADD and cannot focus on anything in the moment because you have too many "ants in your pants" to do so and it is just so hard . . . then you are an **apprentice.**

48

— If you absolutely believe that staying centered in the present is the best—if you could only remember to do so; usually just live and let live, leaving yesterday and tomorrow to take care of themselves; occasionally worry but figure things will work out; or take life easily and slowly and fully enjoy today . . . then you are in the **journeyman** phase.

— If you live by the motto "Que será, será. Whatever will be, will be," give people and things your full attention in the moment; never overschedule or lament or dwell on the past; or look forward to each day as a brand-new opportunity for you to freely create whatever you want . . . then you are well on your way to **mastering** this lesson and enjoying a relatively stress-free life.

If You Are a **Student** . . .

- Stop talking about the past.

- Keep conversations focused on what is happening
  right now.

- Avoid discussions about the "future"—especially those
  that are full of doom and gloom.

- Once an hour, stop and notice out loud something that
  is right in front of you in the here and now—such as
  a calendar, a clock, the weather, or the people you are
  with—then say, "I am here and all is well."

- Practice breathing slowly.

- Focus on one thing for a few minutes every hour, such as
  a great cup of tea, the weather, the chair you are sitting
  on, or the conversation you are having.

If You Are an **Apprentice** . . .

- Get off public transportation or park your car a few blocks away from your job, and walk the rest of the way, noticing what is going on in the streets.

- Keep phone conversations focused on the present and cut them short if they drift into the disappointing past or scary future.

- Talk only about what exists today—no matter how unimportant it may feel in the face of the daunting future or the oppressive past.

- Ask your Creator to help you remain centered on this day.

If You Are a **Journeyman** . . .

- Whenever you drift backward into the past or forward into the future, laugh and ask God to take over.

- Be fully present. What are you doing? How do you feel? Do more of that.

- Record a greeting on your answering machine or cell phone that says, "Leave me a present by telling me something marvelous about *today.* Past and future need not reply."

- Seek support and fellowship in organizations whose philosophy is to live one day at a time, and work closely with them.

If You Are on Your Way to **Mastering** this Lesson . . .

- Take your time at breakfast and savor your morning's start.

- Move through your day at a gentle pace, enjoying the people you meet.

- Breathe deeply, slowly, and often.

- Enjoy how much time, space, and inner peace comes with being in the moment.

Your Soul's Lesson
Live in the Present

Your Soul's Purpose
*To Demonstrate the Power That Derives
from Living in the Moment*

Divine Energy Flows Through You, Not From You

The power to create flows through you, not from you. This force comes from your Higher Divine Self, not from your personal ego. That part of yourself blocks manifestation while your Essential Being channels it.

Your Inner Intelligence is your power source, and it gives you the energy and ability to express your full creative potential. Setting your ego aside and connecting to your Sacred Consciousness plugs you into your wellspring of ideas, possibilities, and abundance.

This can be a challenging concept to grasp, and one I had trouble with myself when it was first introduced to me years ago. For one thing, I had a very healthy sense of myself and my ego, and didn't like the idea of having to stop being who I was in order to fulfill my highest creative promise. My teacher, a wonderful metaphysician and intuitive named Charlie Goodman, laughed at me when I voiced my resistance. Irritated, I asked him how he found that funny. He walked over to the closet and pulled out a beautiful old lamp that was stored there and set it on the floor in front of me.

"What do you think of this?" he asked, still chuckling.

Not fully understanding what he was doing and why it was relevant to my question, I reluctantly answered, "I think it's lovely," admiring the ornate brass etchings around the base and the teardrop crystals dangling from the top.

"I think so, too," he agreed.

"So why is it in your closet instead of in the living room where it can be seen and used?" I asked.

"That's a good question," he replied. "Why don't you plug it in and set it over there on that table."

Lifting it off the floor and wondering what this was all about, I gingerly placed it in front of me on the end table and then reached over to the cord, only to find that the plug was missing.

"Wait a minute, Charlie," I said, not sure he was aware of this. "There isn't a plug at the end of this cord, so I can't turn it on. Without it, the lamp won't work."

"Exactly," he stated. "No matter how beautiful this object is, unless it's connected to an energy source, it can't express what it was made for, can it?"

"Of course not. It's useless," I said, thinking that such a gorgeous antique with no way to make it work was ridiculous.

"As handsome as it is, it was designed for energy to flow through it so that it could turn on and properly light the room," he explained. "In a way, we're no different from this lamp as we, too, are lovely creations who are also engineered to allow a higher energy source to move through us."

You have the ability to manifest things because you channel Divine Power. As a co-creator with the Universe, you have been given the power to set up the perfect conditions for creativity to flow, but it comes through you from the Higher Self—not from your ego or personal will.

Reflect on the forces in nature. For example, when you choose to cultivate a garden, you select the flowers and plants, pick the location, till the soil, put the seeds in the earth, and protect them while they germinate. But you do not personally grow anything. Divine Spirit moving *through* nature causes the garden to blossom. You provide the ideal conditions for the plants to thrive, but for the process to succeed, you must then step aside and let Sacred Intelligence do its work.

Apply these same rules to all your creations. You can use your intelligence, emotions, and imagination to shape and form something you desire, but then you must turn to your Inner Wisdom in order to manifest it. Your ego can watch and learn, but it cannot direct the process.

Perhaps you have spontaneously experienced the creative power of your Higher Self expressing through you. When you move aside, whether consciously or unconsciously, and allow this Greater Consciousness to take over, an incredible force larger than you awakens and assumes control.

I experience the power of my Higher Self whenever I'm speaking publicly. Normally a low-key, quiet, introverted person, the minute I'm in front of a class or up onstage, my ego disappears completely, and my Divine Essence kicks in with an unbelievable strength. I feel as though I'm 50 feet tall and fearless. I lose all anxiety; and instead find my heart filled with love, enthusiasm, intention, and joy. The words flow from some place other than my brain and often surprise me. It's an incredible and wonderful thing to experience.

When my Sacred Self takes over, my intuitive perceptions become razor sharp. I'm not just talking to people—I feel their spirits and connect with them directly. There's no way that this type of communication can be rehearsed or prepared. Instead, I just show up, become receptive to my Inner Knowing, open my mouth, and see what comes through. At times I feel a little nervous beforehand, but because I trust my Soul Wisdom to be the speaker, I don't give my ego's anxieties too much attention. I've learned that I don't have to worry because my Higher Consciousness never disappoints.

I've met other speakers who say that they've experienced the same connection I have. Wayne Dyer, for instance, is a man who speaks from the flow of his Higher Self. I know this because when he gives talks, I feel it. Anthropologist and author Jean Houston and the comedian Robin Williams (one of my favorite people in the world), also allow their Divine Spirits to move through them. My dear friend, artist Julia Cameron, once found herself suddenly writing an opera based on the explorer Magellan. Immersed in it for days, when she stopped for a break, her shell-shocked ego objected loudly, saying, "Who do you think you are, Julia, writing an opera!? You can't do that!"

Her Higher Self calmly responded, "You're a musician, and I'm showing you how to write an opera."

Many great inventors and artists have said that their best ideas simply dropped into their minds, as though handed to them. Edison's lightbulb first turned on in his head. Einstein's theory of relativity and Leonardo da Vinci's design for an airplane were also all gifts from the Sacred Consciousness.

All important innovations in art, music, and even science have been manifested through the Higher Self. It is your link between unlimited Divine potential and your personal latent abilities. When you recognize and allow the power of this Light to flow through you, your creative possibilities become limitless.

My daughter Sonia recently went out to lunch with international rock star Billy Corgan, who happens to be a family friend. Normally, he's a low-key, extremely shy, and reserved man, so she couldn't figure out how he transforms into such a formidable presence onstage. Sonia asked him how he does it and how he feels when he performs.

He sat quietly for a moment, and then said, "I walk out in my normal awareness and personality, yet the minute I see the audience and hit that first chord on the guitar, another force descends upon me and completely takes over. It's me, but not my 'small me.' Instead, I feel that it's me at my greatest unleashed potential. In that space, I believe that I can do anything. When the show's over, this energy subsides, and I'm back to being the quiet me."

I understand what he's saying because I experience the same shift every time I sit down to do a psychic reading for someone. Even after 30 years, I still walk into my office wondering if I'll be able to offer insight to that person. I worry about whether I'll have anything to say, and hope and pray that I can find a connection that's worthwhile. I'm not sure—or at least the small me isn't. Yet the moment I see my clients, or hear their voices on the phone, a profound change occurs. My ego completely disappears, and only my Higher Self is present and does the reading. It's so thorough a shift that when I'm finished, I often don't even remember what I said. My ego wasn't there, so I didn't hear the message.

Without the Divine Inner Being, very little or nothing gets accomplished—at least nothing truly creative, empowering, or filled with light and brilliance. Without the Core Power in charge, you remain trapped in yesterday's creations instead of fulfilling today's dreams.

My client Jerry came to see me for the third time in a year, struggling at each point with the same issue and frustration. Miserably employed, he wanted to quit his job and begin his own business, perhaps a small café. He thought about it continually but couldn't get beyond the fear of committing. Although I assured him that the idea was an excellent one and that if he proceeded, it would work out, he wouldn't let himself believe me. Or more accurately, his small self—his ego—wouldn't let him have faith in his dream. He argued against the idea the entire time we were together:

"How can I be sure that this is the thing to do? Cafés come and go every day! If I open one, it will take all my money and I'll have nothing to fall back on. I don't even cook. What would I serve? Why would people come to my restaurant? It's just a dumb idea, and I can't believe I'm even asking about it."

All his hesitations clearly revealed that his Higher Self was allowed no part in his intention.

"Jerry," I asserted, "for the umpteenth time, you can do this! Just get out of your own way and let your Inner Wisdom take over."

Every time I said that, an ever-so-faint glimmer of light crossed his face. Then, bam! His ego would wrestle him to the ground once again.

"That's well and good to say," he'd argue, "when money isn't involved, but in real matters you have to be practical."

It was a waste of time trying to convince Jerry of the possibility for success. In his case, there wasn't any—not as long as he believed that his ego would create it. The only thing that his "small me" produced was misery and more unhappiness, and he couldn't see it. It shot down every idea he had and blatantly dismissed his Divine Essence as a fabricated notion that was nice to think about but wasn't real.

Finally, I said, "Jerry, I can't lie to you, you're absolutely right. With this approach, you won't succeed in opening a café or anything else. Until you realize that you are spirit, a creative being, and invite your Higher Self to lead the way, nothing is going to happen. Nothing at all."

When he heard that, it was as if I'd thrown cold water in his face. "You mean this is it? I thought you said that I'd achieve my dream."

"No," I said, "you can't create a flourishing café, at least as long as you let your ego dominate and shut out your Greater Consciousness. So you might as well give up and get used to your suffering because it isn't going to change—and you know it."

Jerry was stunned into silence. I just smiled and sent him love. We both sat quietly for five full minutes. Then he got up and started for the door.

"Nothing will change?" he asked one more time.

"No, not unless you turn things over to your Higher Self. Good luck."

He nodded thoughtfully, then left.

I don't know what Jerry will do next. We learn soul lessons at our own pace, and this one was especially hard for him. I had compassion but knew that there was nothing more I could do. We can share the knowledge we've gained with one another, talk about our successes, offer encouragement, and cheer each other on, but we have to master these lessons through our own initiative. I knew that I'd been able to help Jerry a little by telling him what he must do—surrender his ego and allow his Higher Self to create. Beyond that, he has to decide for himself when he's ready to take the next step.

Instead of manifesting anything new, your ego repeats patterns. This is not creative. You continue to experience the same disappointing relationships, money problems, health issues, dead-end jobs, boredom, unhappiness, and misery you already know. The ego is quite masterful in re-creating these loveless, lifeless ruts. The only way to break through them and tap into your Divine Power is to turn every intention and vision over to your Spiritual Source immediately, and keep them there.

Affirm daily: "Higher Self, I leave it to you. I am your faithful servant and open to your way." Then allow it. Relax, let go, be open, and trust this sacred part of you to do the work. The minute you learn this, you will never again be burdened by your mind. Nor will you be stumped or arrested in the pursuit of your desires. Your Internal Wisdom will find the way and the means to fulfill your creative intention. You simply need to follow its guidance.

Now you can apply the lesson.

— If you have never heard of your Higher Self, find the idea of turning your ego over to a greater power strange; are so controlling that you cannot imagine surrendering anything; or lie awake at night with your mind going in circles, trying to figure everything out in all manner of ways, but to no avail . . . then you are a **student** in working with this lesson.

— If you have heard of the concept of a Divine Inner Being and find it a comforting thought but are reluctant to put any serious faith in it; appreciate the idea of having a Sacred Power yet worry far too much to ever let it take over; accept that you have a Greater Consciousness but have to be sure of how things work before you will trust it . . . then you are an **apprentice.**

— If you know that your Higher Self is a genuine power and have experienced it taking over from time to time; find yourself worrying and thinking less and having more trust that your Inner Wisdom will handle life; feel bursts of inspiration; discover the desire and courage to follow your intuition and then surprise yourself again and again with how creative you are; sense the presence of your Sacred Source and ask for its help . . . then you are a **journeyman.**

— If you are fearless in your vision and find power, courage, willingness, and joy in being certain that your Higher Self will deliver; know in your heart that what you focus on will come to pass if you leave it to your Divine Soul; feel unlimited in your creative possibilities and trust your Essential Intelligence; or sleep peacefully at night and wake up with uplifting, inspiring ideas . . . then you are on your way to **mastering** this lesson and living in unbridled freedom.

If You Are a Student . . .

- Remember that you have a Higher Self.

- Start asking your Inner Wisdom to take over.

- Give your controlling ego a pet name like "Worry Wart" or "Poindexter," and lovingly ask it to be quiet.

If You Are an **Apprentice** . . .

- Visit museums, study architecturally significant buildings, walk through an arboretum, and listen to moving music, and see if you notice the Divine forces present in these works.

- Ask your Greater Consciousness to maintain direct contact with you by giving you peaceful feelings.

- Notice how strong your ego is and practice laughing at yourself (lovingly, of course) to help ease its grip.

- Repeat the daily affirmation: "Higher Self, use my mind, heart, and body to serve humanity and create to my fullest potential," or write a similar one of your own.

If You Are a **Journeyman** . . .

- Intentionally let your Higher Self take over at work by brainstorming, relaxing control, playing, and praying.

- Notice the vibration of your Sacred Soul, not only in yourself, but in others as well.

- Count your enlightened empowered moments for 24 hours, and ask your Higher Self to double these every day.

- Bend, flex, take a yoga class, or dance to the music of your favorite band—anything that gets you to move and loosens your ego's tight hold on you a little more.

If You Are on Your Way to **Mastering** this Lesson . . .

- Thank your Inner Wisdom daily for its continual flow of support and blessings, and notice how this multiplies them.

- Ask your Divine Essence to feed you new and creative ideas every hour, and voice them as they arise.

- Thoroughly surrender to your Higher Self; and give your thinking, controlling, worrying mind a permanent vacation.

Your Soul's Lesson
Turn Everything Over to Your Higher Self

Your Soul's Purpose
To Allow Your Higher Self to Lead Your Life

Refine Your Reason

Develop your faculty of reason, your capacity to think logically and be objective. Look at life beyond your emotional and subjective filters to see what is true in front of you now. Used properly, the intellect is a powerful tool of awareness that supports your soul's evolution. It is the channel through which you view the world and interpret it. Nothing supports your intuitive consciousness and spiritual development more thoroughly than a sharp, analytical, rational mind—one that observes carefully, records accurately, and distills information properly.

Problems arise when you confuse objective reason with illogical or automatic conclusions, biases, and assertions—or with other people's opinions. This is a common error.

I had a client, Joe, who had continual trouble finding and keeping solid employees for his painting business. Drawing from a talent pool of mostly Dominican and Ecuadorian immigrants, he was convinced that they all worked well for several months, then messed up, lost interest, left, or had to be fired.

"It happens every time," he said. "By six months, the party's over. I can count on it. I haven't had a single person work for me for more than half a year. As a reasonable business owner, I use this awareness. I'm always out looking for new laborers to replace the old ones. That way, I won't get stuck. It's tiring, but smart."

The way Joe explained it, it did sound like a rational plan, at least on the surface. People can be desperate for jobs, especially new immigrants. Of course they'd be eager to get employment as soon as possible. But after they settle down and their lives become a little more stable, it would seem inevitable that they'd start to question whether they like their work and that they'd eventually lose interest in it.

And yet, when I looked a little deeper, I could see that Joe's so-called reasoning was nothing more than his own projections manipulating his workers into getting discouraged and quitting. Although unaware of his maneuvers, he was the reason that they left. In the beginning, he was very kind but strict because he wanted them to succeed. He knew that this approach was the best way to gain their trust and quiet their fears.

However, after they'd been on the job around four or five months—just before it was time to give them a raise—Joe started being more demanding, hypercritical, vague about scheduling, and tardy with their paychecks. He was less considerate and respectful; spoke in a harsher tone to his employees than when he'd hired them, often yelling at them when he shouldn't have; and became careless about keeping accurate track of their hours. It was no wonder they left their jobs at this juncture.

I told him to stop the behavior that provoked such a high turnover and instead strive to develop a sense of pride and security among his employees, which would stabilize the work place. I suggested that he stop being condescending to his staff or writing them off just because his inner clock said it was time to get rid of them.

My insights were eye-opening for him. "You may have a point there," he said. "I never considered that I'm the problem. I'll give it some thought."

He went home, studied his behavior toward his employees, tried some new techniques, and, not surprisingly, reduced the number of people quitting by 50 percent.

"When I started this business," he remarked, "several contractors told me to expect a high turnover, so I figured that they knew something I didn't. I assumed that they were right, and therefore I didn't question it. What I was unaware of is how their opinions influenced my behavior to make them right."

Reason becomes blocked when you react emotionally to a situation. Detach from your feelings and study the facts before you respond. Armed with sound and accurate information, you can change any circumstance and send it in a new direction. Without such data, you are powerless.

To develop sound objective-thinking skills, carefully observe your world without bias. Be aware of your tendency to cloud your intellect by approaching situations or other people while holding strong (though often unconscious) projections that distort the truth.

I have a client who works for the IRS who's kind, grounded, and generous to a fault. And yet the minute someone hears where she works, she's immediately categorized as "the enemy" and treated poorly. As much as she loves her job (and she's helped many people with tax troubles), it's her greatest sorrow as well because she's so projected upon and hated.

Sound reason can only be cultivated with an open mind. Often, when others, your Higher Self, or your guides offer you an idea or a solution to a problem, you cast it aside without reasonable consideration because it is unfamiliar or different.

I spoke with a client last year who was starting a day spa in the northern suburbs of Chicago and wanted to do something original to attract customers and get the business going. I was guided to suggest that she offer intuitive readings, color therapy, and aura balancing as part of her services.

She immediately raised her hand in protest and said, "Give me something sensible." In spite of my assurances that such sessions and healings are in high demand in health resorts these days, and even though I cited several well-known facilities around the country that offer these benefits, she smiled blankly and stopped listening. Her mind was firmly closed to this proposition, and she wouldn't budge. Intuitive readings and alternative practitioners were too weird and risky to consider in her shop.

"I'm only suggesting something that could attract customers in answer to your question," I repeated, giving it one last try.

She again dismissed the idea. She wasn't open, so I stopped recommending such services and said, "Well, then, word of mouth will have to do, as you don't have a budget for advertising."

Shaking her head on the way out the door and laughing at what she considered "my crazy notion, especially for the upscale North Shore neighborhood," she invited me to her grand opening, but I wasn't able to go.

Eight months later, I received an emergency phone call from her ask-ing if I could see her immediately. When she arrived, she looked pained. She said that another day spa had been established within a mile of hers and was taking all of her business. It was so bad that she feared she might have to close. When I asked if she'd studied what might be going on over there to create such a draw, she replied that in addition to standard spa fare, the center offers all kinds of New Age treatments, such as aura cleansing, intuitive readings, and Reiki energy therapies.

"Apparently they're all the rage. If only I had known!" she lamented.

I looked at her incredulously. Not only had she dismissed my sug-gestion that her business offer these services, she'd done it so thoroughly that she didn't even remember her prior reading with me.

A closed mind is death to your creative power. The ego can become so rigid and fixed in its perceptions that it unreason-ably filters out the truth of the current situation and emerging information.

The worst display of this editing of reality that I ever witnessed was when a gay client arrived for a reading with his lover, a man clearly sick and near death. The minute he entered my office, he said to me, "Under no uncertain terms do we want to hear anything bad. We're only inter-ested in getting good news today. Of course, I'm sure that's all you'll have to offer anyway."

Respecting his wishes, and realizing the futility of going against his unreasonably closed mind, I avoided the subject of his partner's failing health and the consequential need to prepare for his passing, and instead focused on other topics. It felt as though I were pretending that an enor-mous elephant in the middle of the room wasn't there, but I had to work within the parameters I'd been given. It seemed almost ridiculous to me to concentrate on the insignificant, but this was evidently what they wanted me to do.

Six weeks later, when his lover suddenly collapsed and was hospital-ized, my client called me again, shocked and in utter disbelief.

"Couldn't you have foreseen this and warned me?" he asked angrily. "Had you done your job correctly, my partner might have been able to avoid this disaster."

It's hard to believe that people can be so illogical, but they can. I know that I've been that way at times, and so have you. We're all guilty of letting our emotions override our reason.

Your Higher Self directs you, but if you cloud the channel with emotionally charged inaccuracies, poor perceptions, and biased notions, you will not be able to access it. Instead, you will end up drowning in drama and confusion. Only when you become calmly observant can you receive clear, direct, intuitive guidance from your Inner Wisdom.

One of my best and dearest friends, Joan Smith, recently experienced a serious and challenging need to receive clear communication from her Higher Reason. Unexpectedly struck by a severe seizure last fall, she was rushed off to the hospital, where, after a series of tests, she was diagnosed with a brain tumor. A short time later she underwent surgery, only to have the doctors find stage IV cancer. She was given a bleak prognosis and left to handle this horrific scenario on her own.

The first thing Joan did was immediately begin to learn everything she could about her condition, as well as every treatment known, including both mainstream medical modalities and alternative and complementary therapies. The pursuit kept her grounded and prevented her from collapsing into sheer terror. Step-by-step, armed with cutting-edge information, she created a personal healing plan. The more she knew about her cancer, the clearer her intuition became on how best to deal with it.

The key, she said, was discerning fact from opinion. Some of her doctors didn't think that she could survive, while others saw it very differently. Joan immediately distanced herself from those who weren't optimistic, as she'd found evidence that a negative health-care provider is lethal to a patient's chances for survival.

After informing herself about the pros and cons of chemotherapy, she chose to forego it and instead pursue alternative treatments because her gut told her to do so. Many people dismissed her proactive intuitive decisions as crazy and reckless, but others supported her. How are her choices working out? As I write this, her last brain scan showed that she was cancer free.

Observe and acknowledge everything, including your feelings, but do not let them overwhelm you. They are intense, and in the throes of a heated reaction, nothing is obvious. However, they do die down eventually. It is too difficult to remain in such a heightened state all the time. The physical body tires of strong emotions and the adrenaline they send coursing through it, and you shut them off when you reach the saturation point. Never assess a situation or decide on a course of action when you are caught up in the moment. Your perceptions will be inaccurate, and your access to your Higher Self will be blocked. Let the winds of emotion blow by, for only then will you be able to see clearly and act wisely and creatively.

You have blind spots, places where you are unable to see the bigger picture as a result of your upbringing, social conditioning, and even past lives. It is your soul's lesson to remove these barriers to reason. Be willing to see what has been hidden from you. Where is your reason stymied due to the inability or resistance to looking at the greater scheme of things as objectively and accurately as possible? What habitual emotional responses close off access to your Inner Wisdom? Ponder these questions and your Greater Consciousness will show you the answers.

Ignore your ego's view. It is defensive, narrow, subjective, self-righteous, judgmental, insecure, angry, and fearful. Look at life from your Higher Self's point of view instead—one that is calm, objective, creative, solution driven, nonjudgmental, and loving.

This is tricky. I look up and see a pile of papers, an empty Starbucks coffee cup, books strewn across a table, and the remnants of birthday-present wrapping from a gift I received from my friend Lilly. My first emotional reaction is: "I see a mess and I must clean it up." My second observation is: "I see a comfortable workspace and I enjoy it." Which is true? Probably both.

Poorly developed reason is often a consequence of inadequate sight—not just eyesight, although that does play a part, but also insight and observation. Have you ever heard the saying "You see only what you want to see"? Whether you put on rose-colored glasses, filtering out all unpleasantness; or perceive the world as a glass half empty, seeing only the dark and negative aspects of situations, neither approach gives you an accurate picture of reality, and therefore you remain unable to change it.

Check your eyesight so that you can see clearly. If your vision is not sharp, then your reason will not be either. Focus your observations so that you have an unclouded view on all levels. The more objectively you can discern present conditions and the less biased your perception, the more you will have ready access to your Higher Self, which will then lead to positive solutions and effective creations.

One client of mine unreasonably accused his wife of having an affair and asked for a divorce because he observed her in a restaurant kissing another man. Never mind that she was home at the time with their children. He refused to accept her denial and assurance that she wasn't cheating on him and chose to believe his eyes instead. The problem was that he was extremely nearsighted, and although he thought that he'd seen his wife, it was actually her younger sister. He only admitted his mistake and apologized when the sister came to visit three weeks later to introduce her new fiancé, who turned out to be the man in the restaurant. It sounds ridiculous, but don't kid yourself—this kind of thing happens all the time.

Overly emotional reactions compromise your creative efficacy. Do not get intoxicated by your feelings; refuse to allow them to manipulate your perceptions. Vent, feel, express, and listen to your impulses, then quiet down. When all is calm, study the situation again with a clear mind before deciding which course of action to take.

Biases, blind spots, and closed-minded opinions cripple your ability to skillfully manifest what you want. Divine Spirit hides from nothing and judges nothing. Reason, when finely tuned and accurately engaged, is the bridge between what exists now and what you desire for the future.

Now you can apply the lesson.

— If you are an emotional hothead or a leaky faucet of tears; seldom accurately remember the details about people, places, or events; take everything personally and wonder why the world can be so cruel; find yourself stuck in one drama after another, each with a similar scary theme; react without thinking; rush forward too quickly; and make premature judgments more often than not . . . then you are a **student** in learning this lesson.

— If you are highly sensitive to people and things and shut down easily; get your feelings hurt readily; carry other's perspectives way too heavily in your heart; hesitate before you speak and try to think things through before you act, but often fail to see another's point of view; or keep a journal and are considering seeing a therapist to gain deeper perspective . . . then you are an **apprentice.**

— If you never make a decision in haste, but rather take the time to learn all you can before moving forward; call trusted friends and supportive advisors to help you sort through problems when you are not thinking clearly; pay keen attention to people, places, and objects and have a sharp eye for detail; pause to consider before reacting, preferring to talk things over when you are calm; or wait for answers to come to you after learning all you can about something . . . then you are a **journeyman.**

— If you have a nearly photographic memory; observe beyond the surface and feel as though you have insight into things; refrain from drawing conclusions and deciding what to do until you get all the necessary information, sort it out, and sleep on it; have an open mind and are always willing to learn more, especially in those areas in which you consider yourself quite knowledgeable; or pray, meditate, and wait for guidance from your Higher Self . . . then you are on your way to **mastering** this Soul Lesson.

If You Are a **Student** . . .

- Slow down and calm down.

- Get more information and make certain that your sources are objective and reliable before drawing conclusions.

- Notice as many details as you can when you are engaged with people or are in new places.

- Breathe, take a walk or a bath, and relax when you are overly emotional.

If You Are an **Apprentice** . . .

- Join a support group of some kind to get feedback and new perspectives.

- Open your mind and be willing to see beyond your own point of view.

- Search out your blind spots by studying recurring problems with the help of teachers, therapists, and unbiased friends.

- Get your vision checked, have your glasses repaired, and learn exercises to improve your eye muscles.

- Strive to observe new things and more detail about familiar people and places every day.

If You Are a **Journeyman** . . .

- Ask your Higher Self to reveal your blind spots and raise your awareness.

- Do physical and meditative exercises for several minutes a day.

- Count to ten and breathe through dramas and life challenges rather than giving in to them.

- Ask questions, do research, or take a class to find out all you can about a situation, a recurring problem, or an area of creative interest.

- Find trusted life advisors who will listen and help you sort through all the information you gather to get to the clearest, most accurate picture possible.

- Once you have researched and organized your data, turn to your Inner Wisdom for the definitive answer or solution.

If You Are on Your Way to **Mastering** this Lesson . . .

- Read new books about old and favorite subjects.

- When you have a conversation, take in every detail with both your head and heart and ask for more information whenever your spirit suggests it.

- Take regular periods of alone time to ponder, digest, and sort through what you have learned.

- Ultimately turn everything over to your Higher Self for a final decision.

Your Soul's Lesson
Develop and Refine Your Reason

Your Soul's Purpose
Use Higher Reason to See the True Spirit in All People,
Even When at Various Stages

Follow Your Inner Voice

Follow your inner voice—the quiet, guiding expression of your Higher Self. It is found in the heart, the home of the Divine Intelligence in your physical body. Your interior counsel is different from the directives of your ego. It is direct, calm, and clear, and serves not only your own best interests but the good of all persons. It does not flatter or condemn, and never tells you what to do. It only makes gentle suggestions that support your authentic path. It is your soul's compass in this life, and it keeps you from becoming lost in the confusion of the world.

Your inner voice is not a personal one, but is instead your private connection to the Divine Spirit we all share. It is available to guide you at all times. To connect to its wisdom, simply focus on your heart and listen.

In order to truly hear, you must first disengage from other voices. To begin with, stop soliciting opinions from others. It is perfectly fine to seek direction and support from all available resources, but in the end, let your Higher Self be your final and ultimate authority.

Do nothing before consulting your Inner Wisdom. To do this, quiet your mind and place your full attention on your heart. Be patient and allow it to speak. Ask directly for guidance, then listen. The Higher Self is subtle and does not interrupt your ego or the voices of the world. You therefore must tune out the external noise and the nagging words of your ego to hear its gentle direction. If you make this effort, you will always connect with your Source.

Listen to your inner voice with your entire being—with every cell in your body. Have you ever been alone in a house and heard an unfamiliar sound? Can you recall how all the thoughts racing through your mind came to a complete standstill as you were alerted to the potential intruder? This kind of undivided, cellular attention gives you access to your inner voice. The ability to focus on this level is developed through regular periods of quiet reflection, contemplation, and prayer. Start with 5 minutes and gradually increase to 30 minutes a day. This becomes easier—more and more relaxing with practice.

To know if the guidance you receive is indeed that of your Sacred Consciousness, consider how it affects you. Does it leave you feeling at ease with yourself? Peaceful? Rested? Your Essence has a naturally grounding and calming influence. It resonates as truth in every cell in your being.

No one can determine for you whether you are listening to your inner voice or your ego. Part of your soul's work is to make that distinction on your own. However, we can offer clues to help you.

Your Divine Wisdom:

- Affirms your spirit
- Leaves you feeling confident
- Eases your insecurities
- Elicits your compassion and adoration for those around you
- Encourages self-love and acceptance of yourself
- Is honest
- Inspires you to be more generous and courageous

If you do not experience these things, your ego is playing tricks on you. Change the channel because you are tuned in to something that does not serve your soul.

When accessing your Inner Soul's Light, you will face times when you must challenge or override the opinion of others. Do not be afraid. Trust your inner voice and follow it anyway. Doing so ultimately serves everyone.

Recently, as I was driving home from an errand and contemplating writing this portion of the book, I turned on the radio and caught the tail end of a National Public Radio interview. A journalist was speaking with one of the scientists who'd been involved in the Human Genome Project in 2000. The researcher said that when the human genome was first decoded, experts were able to understand about 90 percent of all information about our genetic makeup. The other 10 percent, however, remained a mystery and has been the primary area of study for most geneticists ever since.

One of their most significant breakthroughs came not long ago when they discovered that a huge part of the human genetic structure that had been cast off and ignored as essentially waste turned out to be a mother lode of data, perhaps even the key link to achieving a full understanding of our DNA.

The scientist interviewed said that it was incredible that this section of the genome had originally been overlooked, given its colossal importance. Geneticists everywhere asked themselves how on earth this could have happened, especially as it was the equivalent of missing a huge, white rhinoceros in the middle of a room. Curious, the reporter asked, "Well, how did it happen?"

"Easy," he replied. "Scientists are no different from anyone else. We see what we're trained to observe, and hear what we've been taught to listen for. From one generation to the next, no one questioned the information that was passed on. They simply accepted it as fact—at least, that is, until one of our researchers began to have doubts about it. He said, 'My inner voice told me to check that data, and I did.'"

By listening to his Soul Wisdom, this man hit scientific pay dirt. His guidance helped deepen our understanding of human genetics. Because one person paid attention to his Higher Self instead of outside experts, we've gained some extremely valuable knowledge about human genes.

You have been educated to ignore your Divine Intelligence to such a degree that for many of you, it is automatic and unthinkable to even question the information other people give you. Be mindful of this false indoctrination and pay keen attention to what and to whom you listen—and the power you give to these supposed authorities instead of to your Higher Self. You may not even be aware of how others' opinions silence your inner voice.

I met with a brilliant young man who was working toward his doctorate in art and music history at the University of Chicago. Although he was sharp, intense, and extremely articulate, for the first few minutes of speaking with him, I felt as though I were talking to a robot. His words were short, cold, and canned, and felt rehearsed. I could hear thousands of years of professors, in life after life, speaking through him. I sensed that he was just passing their ideas and values along. These weren't his words, thoughts, personal feelings, or convictions coming from his mouth, but the opinions of others. He had an acquired, contrived self.

I shared my intuitive observations and asked him if he felt or resonated with anything he was saying on a soul level. Surprised to be asked this, he stuttered, then stumbled, laughed, squirmed, and shook his head, as if to dislodge those voices, and finally went absolutely quiet.

Then he said, "Yes. It's true. I'm echoing things I've learned. These aren't my words, thoughts, or any part of me at all. I repeat them because I've been trained to. But I hate that I do this. I don't even know what I think anymore because I'm so invested in impressing my teachers. That's why I'm meeting with you—I don't know if I have a voice of my own."

I sat quietly with him for the next few moments, contemplating his plight and praying for guidance to help him access his Higher Self. At first, all I got was silence. Then suddenly the counsel came—not in sentences but in music. His Inner Being spoke to my heart with the song of his soul, and it was beautiful.

"Your inner voice speaks to you through music," I stated, "not words."

He looked shocked, then was overcome by emotion. Embarrassed, he asked, "Why am I crying?" wiping his eyes as fast as the tears came. "This is so weird. And I can't believe you brought up music. It's my first love—the only place where I'm not bombarded by everyone else's expertise. I love to compose and play the piano, but I rarely do it anymore."

I was guided to be silent. I trusted that he'd hear his Divine Source if I said nothing. After a moment, he relaxed. "Thank you. I got the answer I came for," he said, and left.

Learn to distinguish the voice of your Higher Self from the advice of other discarnate entities, such as spirit guides and nature elementals. Even though they can be helpful, some are mischievous and may mislead you. Specifically, be alert to flattery, as this is their typical way of gaining your attention and confidence. It is always a telltale warning that you are dealing with a low-level being that should be ignored.

A client, Fran, called and said that she was so excited to have finally tapped into her Divine Essence. "You know," she said rather smugly, "my Higher Self said that not everyone is as elevated as I am, and that I'm a special soul."

"How does that make you feel?" I asked.

"Wonderful," she squealed. "Like I won a prize!"

"And if you're so exceptional, what will that get you?" I continued.

"I don't know," she said, puzzled and slightly annoyed that I wasn't exactly thrilled about her entry into the club of psychic elitists. "What do you mean by that?"

"Do you want to be better or different from everyone? Isn't that a bit isolating?"

"I suppose it could be," she conceded.

"Haven't you been complaining of feeling alienated and lonely? How can being so extraordinary serve that?"

"I don't know. Now I'm confused."

"All I know," I said, "is that the true inner voice clarifies—it doesn't complicate. It invites peace and union with the world, not isolation. If I were you, I'd check out the messages you're receiving a little more carefully before I'd be convinced that they're coming from your Higher Self. So far, they don't seem to be producing the right results."

Fran said that I was just jealous and left. I don't know where her voice has led her since we spoke, but I've heard that her pronouncement of being special has pushed away many people who were in her life.

Guides are assigned solely to help you connect to and follow your Higher Self, not to separate you from it or contradict it in any way. Do not listen to anything other than your inner voice. It is the highest, most reliable counsel that you can pursue along your soul's path.

Consult it about all things in your life because it is your most beloved friend. Clear the unwanted noise and external influences so that you can communicate without distraction. When you are ready to connect, you will. Your Higher Self has always been present—you have only withdrawn your attention from it.

Now you can apply the lesson.

— If you cannot discern your inner voice; need the constant bombardment of the TV, radio, iPod, or Internet to fill the quiet; read countless newspapers, magazines, and tabloids, and never question the information they contain; or constantly look to others to tell you what to do . . . then you are a **student** with regard to this lesson.

— If you ask for other people's opinions and seek "expert" advice but do not necessarily follow it; do what your family and friends say but secretly wish that you could break free or run away; are starting to pay attention to your inner feelings and talk about them, but only with "safe" people and never with anyone who may oppose you; or crave more solitude but do not consider it an important priority . . . then you are an **apprentice.**

— If you are tired of listening to others; speak up when you disagree; are making time for yourself even if you have to battle for it; are called to learn to meditate, practice yoga, go on a spiritual retreat, or take a deep soul-reflection course; or suddenly like the sound of silence . . . then you are a **journeyman.**

— If you set aside periods for quiet without exception; check in with your inner voice before making a decision or commitment; listen to and stick with your higher guidance—even if it angers, disappoints, or upsets someone else; are at ease with your spirit, confident that you will be safely led and able to discern all intuitive input that will ensure the good of everyone concerned . . . then you are well on your way to **mastering** this soul lesson and being peacefully guided in life.

If You Are a **Student** . . .

- Refrain from asking anybody and everybody to comment on your life—especially about what you should do.

- Heighten your sensitivity to your Higher Self by listening to a beloved piece of music, and see how many voices and instruments you can discern.

- Avoid mindlessly talking too much, particularly with people you are seeking approval from.

If You Are an **Apprentice** . . .

- Wean yourself from the newspaper, radio, and TV— at least in the morning—and enjoy the quiet instead.

- Be observant when you have conversations and careful not to get swept up in agreeing just to feel like you belong.

- Pay attention to your words. Are you expressing how you genuinely feel and what you believe in, or are you repeating thoughts, ideas, and sentiments that you have acquired from others?

- Ask your inner voice to speak up, and then be polite, patient, and attentive enough to listen.

If You Are a **Journeyman** . . .

- Pray quietly every day.

- Create as much silence in your routines as possible, with the intention to turn within.

- When you have a conversation, listen without expressing your opinion once in a while. Hold your own counsel.

- Check in with your inner voice before offering your viewpoint, commitment, or decision.

- Do not seek for others to approve of your Soul Wisdom. Instead, journal, pray, and contemplate your guidance to achieve further clarity.

If You Are on Your Way to **Mastering** this Lesson . . .

- Begin every day by listening to your Higher Self, and ask it to refuse all input that does not align with your soul path.

- Relax and detach from the opinions and posturing displays of ego from the outside world.

- Create a quiet sanctuary in your home where you can speak directly to your Divine Inner Being.

- Strive to become even more discerning.

- Talk less and listen more.

Your Soul's Lesson
To Listen Only to the Higher Self

Your Soul's Purpose
*To Model the Personal Grace, Power, and Authority
That Comes from Living in Alignment with Your True Spirit*

Open Your Heart

Live with an open heart. You cannot grow on a soul level if it is closed. Staying receptive connects you to your spirit, other people, and our Creator, the Lord of Life. It channels life force into everyone, and honors God. Allowing the flow of positive emotions is your natural way as a Divine Immortal Being.

If your heart is open, you receive and give love freely. You are nonjudgmental and kind, and feel compassion for all people in the world. You cherish life and you experience Heaven's adoration for you. You are also trusting, tolerant, and patient. Most of all, you become more and more courageous, because love is the antidote to fear.

To open your heart, start by loving yourself. You are a treasured child of God, made in the image and likeness of the Divine, which is only love; therefore, you are also only this quality. To know and accept this will naturally make you supremely receptive. The lie your ego tells—and the source of all your pain—is that you are not made of this Holy Spark and consequently are not worthy of it.

When you realize that the opposite is true and that you are here to be and experience love, you begin to dismantle the defenses, blocks, and barriers that keep you from living this purpose. You start to expand beyond limited notions of romantic or personal attachment and evolve toward a more expansive and all-inclusive activation of universal love.

An open heart does not require that you stop having passionate or affectionate relationships with others. Instead, it asks you to cease loving *selectively*, giving your endearment to some while withholding it from some, too. Recognize the goodness or Godliness in all human beings, and honor and embrace that Divinity in everyone. This is a basic part of your purpose on Earth.

If you release your defenses, you naturally send out a positive, harmonious, peaceful, and caring vibration to the world, which helps stabilize the planet. This energy also eases other people's suffering, which, at its root, is always due to a lack of love.

Your heart has an energetic shield that you can engage to protect you whenever you are subjected to extreme pain, anxiety, or fear. This is useful when you are facing trauma, but it is not intended to be kept in place permanently. If you erect such armor—even when it is called for—you cut your soul off from everything, including your Creator, your Source. We advise you to close your heart only under severe circumstances, and even then only for the shortest period of time possible. To stay receptive under duress, pray for support from God, angels, and guides; and forgive those who hurt you. Letting go of blame safeguards your feeling nature better than anything and heals all wounds.

Andrew and his wife had only one child, Natalie, who was brutally raped and murdered when she was only seven years old. Nearly insane with grief and rage, not only did Andrew have to endure the unthinkable loss of his daughter, he also had to go to court multiple times.

His marriage crumbled under the weight of his despair, and he and his wife divorced. Eventually the man accused of the murder—whom he had hated intensely for so long—turned out to be innocent and was exonerated through DNA evidence. Several years later, another man confessed and was convicted. The desolation, pain, and confusion of all this nearly killed Andrew.

Through the help and love of those close to him, he found the courage to forgive and open his heart once again. Rather than continue to poison himself with hatred and contempt, he chose to turn his situation over to God and get back to living. He and his wife, with whom he'd stayed in contact, remarried and started over. These incredibly momentous decisions gave Andrew his life back. He now speaks to people everywhere about the power of the open heart and forgiveness. It healed both him and his wife, and together they are helping others.

An outpouring of pure adoration is the most potent healing vibration on Earth. With an open heart, every obstacle in your life eventually gives way, because nothing in the world can resist this energy indefinitely. Love recruits support and enthusiasm from every corner of the planet and the Universe. It is also the secret to charismatic power, for the more you love, the more energetically attractive you become. You therefore begin to draw everything that you need directly to you.

You may have experienced many moments when you loved others without reserve. Your heart opens readily to those closest to you—your family, children, and intimate friends. It is also receptive to people you are naturally attracted to—those who appeal to your outer senses (including your eyes) and flatter your ego. These experiences begin to encourage you to love more deeply and broadly. Each positive encounter opens you a little more, until eventually you learn to embrace all humanity as your family.

You become more and more receptive when the ego is no longer the primary guiding voice in your life, but rather, when you are led by your Higher Self.

Reflect on the feeling of pure, receptive love. For example, imagine the birth of a baby. From the moment you first set your eyes upon a newborn, your heart is moved and opens immediately.

A beloved pet has a similar effect. Animals are extremely effective in removing your defenses and seducing you into fully opening up your feeling center because they give you unconditional affection and devotion. Even the most hardened and self-protective people soften and warm to such powerful emotions.

I experienced the power of animals to open the heart several years ago when my own beloved miniature poodle, Miss T, ate an entire box of Frango chocolate mints, which my husband, Patrick, had given to me for Mother's Day. She had to be rushed to the veterinary emergency room to have her stomach pumped because chocolate is lethal to dogs.

When Patrick and I arrived, the waiting room was filled with distressed people of all types and their sick pets. The most impressive part of that experience for me was watching how everyone interacted despite their obvious social differences.

We went to the only animal hospital open at the time, which was on the west side of Chicago, not far from a well-known gang-infested area. Walking in with my sick poodle with her chocolate-minty breath, the first person I encountered was an angry-looking, bearded, tattooed, young man with a scar across his left eye, holding on to a bleeding pit bull. Next to him sat an older, disheveled woman who smelled strongly of urine and alcohol; and on her lap sat a large, shabby, listless Persian cat. The next two chairs were taken by an elderly couple with a small, wheezing, nearly hairless Pekinese who appeared to be on his last legs.

Since there was only one vet on call that night, we were told by the front-desk attendant to settle in for a long wait. We sat in silence for a while, each of us filled with tension and fear for our pets.

Eventually Patrick got bored and started talking to the other people, asking the scruffy man what had happened to his dog. He replied that his pit bull had been in a fight earlier that night and nearly lost his left eye and ear. Next, the lady with the cat described how it had swallowed a needle and needed surgery to remove it or it could puncture the feline's intestines and kill her. Then the older couple spoke about their Pekinese and said that it was simply old and asthmatic . . . and that he was probably going to be put to sleep that night. We then confessed that our Miss T had eaten a whole box of chocolate mints, and everyone laughed.

As we each expressed our concern for our animals, everyone's facades and defenses dropped, and we instantly bonded. For the next three hours, we shared personal stories, told pet tales, exchanged names, and came to care about each others' experiences. We stopped seeing one another as different because it was obvious that beyond our outer appearances, we were the same. We were all just scared animal owners who loved our furry friends and wanted them to be well. By the time the evening ended, we had love for each other, too.

Eventually we all went home with our pets, reassured and relieved (except, of course, the older couple with the Pekinese). We cried and thanked our lucky stars it wasn't our beloved companion that might be put to sleep. With our hearts wide open, the real healing in those hours was our own.

The ability to allow the flow of emotions becomes more challenging as you experience tremendous loss, pain, or abuse in this or past incarnations. When a person undergoes a sudden trauma, the soul can become fragmented and actually leave the body in pieces—thus the expression "I was shattered." This is actually a quite accurate description of what happens when your Divine Essence is seriously injured. When it splinters and exits the physical self, your heart shuts down.

My client Ellen suffered many brutal beatings from an angry and violent stepmother when she was a child. This torment fragmented her soul and closed her heart completely. When I first met her, I felt as though I were speaking to a cold steel door. My words bounced off her defensive sheath as she sat, stoic and oblivious to the world. She was so distant that it was hard to even talk to her.

Ellen had completely isolated herself, yet couldn't understand why she had no luck in love. She wondered why people—men and women alike—moved away from her so quickly. She was hurt by it, all the while unconscious of how her closed heart affected those around her.

Although she was extremely beautiful, hardly anyone wanted to be close to her because her vibration was so lifeless and loveless. It took a lot of care, including therapy, massage, bodywork, spiritual counseling, and prayer to call her divided soul back into her body and for her to become receptive to others again. Ellen even underwent specific sessions for retrieving her Inner Source and restoring it to wholeness before she began to become aware of her heart. With time, effort, and the grace of God, however, her energetic core began to heal and open once again.

What really helped her turn the corner was joining a support network for abused teenage girls. In guiding them through their traumas, she healed herself, and day by day her heart opened a little more. Within weeks, she fell in love with the process of encouraging these young women. She pulled back her defensive shield and developed soul wisdom. Ellen used her experience to show them how to regain their own feeling natures.

It is obvious when people's hearts are shut down and they are not in their body because their eyes are dull and their energy feels stiff, cold, dense, or empty. They have no warmth. If the ego is in control, the jaw is usually clenched, the lips are pursed, the arms are folded or stiff, and the eyes do not make contact.

You can call your soul back into your body through the power of intention; set healthy boundaries around yourself to create a safe vessel in which your spirit can reside. You may also retrieve your Essence through movement, exercise, and physical activity. This raises the vibration of the body, flushes out negative energies that are attached to it, and makes a clear space for the soul to return to. However, the greatest and most powerful way to recover this lost part of yourself is through self-love.

The spirit in you is greater than any injury you have ever experienced. Once you connect and identify with this essential aspect as the real you, it recollects its lost pieces and begins to fully return.

To call your soul home, tap into your Divine light, love yourself, and claim your right to live peacefully in your body, free from invasion by others.

Because your cells carry memory patterns of past injuries, bodywork such as massage therapy, Reiki, healing touch, and reflexology are extremely effective for clearing those imprints and paving the way for your Sacred Essence to return.

Another powerful tool for opening the heart is to forgive those who have hurt you. This feels like an impossible assignment for the false self, the ego that holds on to injuries forever. However, this is not an activity of the ego, but a gift of the spirit. Have you ever heard the saying "To err is human, to forgive divine"? It is true: When you absolve someone, you gain access to your Divine Immortal Self. You release yourself from the dark chains of your ego—and of anyone else's. The more you connect with Inner Wisdom, the stronger your soul becomes, so letting go of blame not only becomes possible, but something you desire.

Forgive yourself for forgetting that you are a Light Being and for allowing yourself to be manipulated and influenced by the ego-based projections you encountered or put forth as you were learning to love. We notice that it is easier for you to forgive others than yourself. Self-judgment is the last vestige of the ego as it tries to exert control and keep you from expanding your soul. Releasing yourself from this criticism is an indication that you are advancing to higher levels of awareness.

Forgiving yourself comes more easily with prayer and a connection to your Higher Self. The ability to readily let go and rarely take offense is one of the greatest demonstrations that you are mastering your soul's lessons.

The final step to opening the heart is to view everything and everyone from the perspective of your Greater Consciousness and realize that you are all students struggling to be free of your fragile and insecure egos. You are at various levels and degrees of awakening to this teaching, so take nothing personally. Recognize the shared struggle and common pain that humans undergo as they grow their souls. See others with the eyes of spirit and never again through the lens of the ego.

View everything and everyone with compassion and love, beginning with yourself. Separate behavior from people, loving them and forgiving their actions. No longer lash out, condemn, or hurt others out of fear. If you do have a lapse of judgment, step back from the offending situation and reconnect with your Divine Essence.

The most inspiring and open-hearted person I know is my own mother. She wasn't always this way, but many years ago she resolved to live with an open heart. Since then, she doesn't judge anyone, including herself, and sees only the spirit within all of us. Her commitment to this is so strong that you could tell her that you're an ax murderer and I'm sure that she would still love and embrace you wholeheartedly and without hesitation.

I asked her recently how she managed to live this way. She replied that it was the most selfish thing she's ever done. From the moment she chose to open her heart to all God's creations—including herself—and see only the Divine in everyone, her pain went away. All the indignities and suffering she'd endured and inflicted that had kept her from sleeping peacefully at night subsided, then disappeared. She said, "I'm peaceful, and for that, the decision to live in this manner—with all its challenges—is worth it."

An open heart is the gateway to peace, and achieving this receptivity is a strong sign that your soul is growing tremendously.

Every step you take on this path is significant and powerfully healing for both you and the planet.

Now you can apply the lesson.

— If you are much too hurt and angry to ever take the chance to be open to anyone; feel cold, shut down, inadequate, detached, and disconnected from your heart; are suspicious, jealous or competitive; hold grudges; speak negatively of others; take pleasure in other people's struggles; or hide your feelings and criticize yourself . . . then you are a **student** in learning this lesson.

— If you want to get over the past and forgive and forget but do not quite know where to begin; would like to behave kindly toward people but easily become intimidated and insecure; are starting to be less critical and have a more positive self-assessment; are getting tired of holding a dim view of life and want to enjoy it, yourself, and others more; or are actively examining your defensive behaviors . . . then you are an **apprentice.**

— If you are actively engaged in coming to terms with the past and letting go of old wounds; are committed to learning to be kinder and more compassionate with yourself and others; are interested and dedicated to seeing the best in people and being honest about your own faults; or are slow to take offense, quick to forgive, and *forget* slights, hurts, and injuries even more rapidly . . . then you are a **journeyman.**

— If you find that life is too short to be critical, judgmental, or blaming; really enjoy people and look for what is positive and good in everyone—and say so; never take personal offense when someone misbehaves or does something harmful; pray for those who are truly deviant; are always the first to say "I'm sorry"; love the human spirit; champion people; or see what is fabulous and have compassion and humor for what is not . . . then you are well on your way to **mastering** this lesson.

If You Are a **Student** . . .

- Get a spiritually based therapist to help you sort through life's ups and downs and challenges.

- Seek the services of a holistic massage therapist or Reiki practitioner on a weekly basis.

- Take up the practice of daily meditation and, if possible, work with a teacher as you learn.

- Seek the support of a group such as a 12-step program to work through the issues of your past and become free to like yourself today.

If You Are an **Apprentice** . . .

- Pray for help in softening your heart and connecting to your Divine Essence.

- Join a spiritual community that centers on love, forgiveness, and nonjudgment.

- Do nurturing things for yourself, such as allowing time for tea, flowers, bubble baths, classical music, and live entertainment.

- Go on a criticism fast.

- Consciously seek lighthearted humor to brighten your view.

If You Are a **Journeyman** . . .

- Recognize the Divine within as pure adoration, and fill your aura with it every morning.

- Consciously practice sending love and light (the vibration of love) to everyone you encounter, especially those who are difficult or injurious to your spirit.

- Lovingly detach and quickly take your leave of situations and people who are provocative, agitated, aggressive, or violent.

- Do not verbally condemn others or yourself. Laugh out loud and allow yourself to enjoy what you adore in life every day.

If You Are on Your Way to **Mastering** this Lesson . . .

- Continue to be kind.

- Be patient, humorous, affectionate, and generous in your appreciation of others.

- Love the amazing, brilliant Spirit in you; and seek to see, engage, and enjoy the luminous Divine Essence in everyone.

Your Soul's Lesson
Open Your Heart

Your Soul's Purpose
Channel More Love into the World

Detach

Detach from the physical world. Be part of the daily activity of life but not enslaved by it. Do not allow your happiness or peace of mind to depend on anything outside of your spirit—including the acquisition of material things, the attainment of fulfilling relationships, or the approval or agreement of others. You should only have faith in following your heart and being true to your Divine Inner Being. You cannot make the Universe around you or the people in it do, feel, or think what you want, no matter how much you may believe that you can persuade others or how hard you may try.

If you are attached to striving to control what you actually cannot in an attempt to achieve joy and a sense of well-being, you are forever doomed. Let go of the need for such manipulation, and do not waste time lamenting or suffering over what is not going your way—nor clinging to notions that circumstances should be other than what they are. Life is what it is.

You may have your preferences and choose to create something else if you do not like what you are experiencing, but do not squander hours agonizing over what is not going your way. Detachment is an attitude that chooses peace of mind over struggling against the world. It means accepting what is without wasting your energy on resistance or wanting things to be different than they are. It is not resignation, but the quiet acceptance of the present reality as you have made it. When you are calm and self-possessed, you preserve your emotions and direct them toward creating what you want rather than against what you do not.

To be detached from the world is a confusing soul lesson for even the most ambitious spiritual student because one of the greatest reasons why you are drawn to a sacred path is that you want to create a more comfortable earthly existence. Asking you to let go of the strong pull of your desires may feel like being brought to a candy store, then told that you cannot have any sweets.

However, freeing yourself of intense yearnings does not suggest that you cannot have treats or anything else that you want on the physical plane. It simply means that you do not allow a fixation on candy—or any other thing, idea, or wish—to destroy your inner peace.

To detach means to choose to have a quiet, content mind no matter what your external conditions are. You are not asked to withdraw, cut yourself off, shut down, push away experiences, or deny yourself the joy of anything. Instead, you are simply required to respond creatively rather than react emotionally to life as it unfolds before you.

One reason why it is important to do this is that as a spiritual being, you eventually leave the physical realm, so you never truly own anything anyway. No matter what you accumulate in this lifetime, when it is time to pass to another dimension through death, you must leave it all behind.

The only real thing worth pursuing in this incarnation is the experience of giving and receiving love. This is the sole aspect of the earthly journey that transcends with you as you transition from one plane to another. The more you love, the more you grow the soul. The root of nonattachment is pure adoration and acceptance.

As long as the ego defines your desires, detachment is impossible. This part of you clings to everything and wants to control it all. Only your spirit—your immortal soul—allows you to break free. When you remember that you are Divine, it is easier, since you know that as a creative being, you are deprived of nothing.

Start by letting go of all unnecessary material objects. It is important to be comfortable and secure, and it is perfectly fine to manifest and enjoy all the beautiful things and experiences on the Earth plane that you desire. Just remember that creating is vital, not having. Do not fall into the trap of *needing* or holding on to what you have drawn into your life too tightly—or painfully grasping fears of not getting what you want—because the price is your peace. The ego loves to keep raising the bar of what you believe you need to feel contented and safe, and it is never satisfied. In fact, ego attachments never allow tranquility. The more you are able to let go of them, changing them to preferences rather than needs, the freer you are to remain serene and undisturbed.

My teacher Charlie, who imparted so much knowledge about the psychic arts to me when I was a young woman, was a very simple man with just a few basic needs. He once told me that he only owned one suit, three shirts, two pairs of trousers, and one pair of shoes. He house-sat for an elderly woman who lived in a nursing home and walked everywhere or took the bus because he didn't own a car. He occupied only two rooms—the bedroom where he slept and the small living room where he did readings and taught classes. He looked shabby and poor, almost like a bum, yet he was extremely comfortable with his unencumbered life and said so all the time.

Moreover, he was also one of the most generous, giving people I've ever known. Nothing about him resonated lack. This was because he wasn't overly invested in material acquisitions and was so detached from everything. He appreciated what he had and acted as though he owned the world and had all of it to share. His freedom from clinging to physical goods made his experience rich.

Conversely, several years later I met a woman named Clare, who came to see me for a reading. She was so wealthy that it was hard to get my mind around how much money she had. She and her husband were real estate developers, and they owned several Chicago lakefront high-rises and office buildings, as well as six seaside hotels in Hawaii. The net worth of these properties was nearly $600 million, and that was only the sum of their investments.

They possessed millions in personal property as well. Needless to say, they had every product imaginable, in all colors, shapes, and styles—not to mention numerous employees and servants who waited on them hand and foot.

You'd think that with so much worldly abundance, Clare would be deliriously happy about her good fortune and blessings. Not so. On the contrary, she was nearly psychotic with fear and worry over her material kingdom. Could she grow it? Would she lose it? Would others try to take it from her? Could she trust her husband? Or should she have a detective spy on him to make certain he wasn't stealing from her?

She asked me all these questions. Her apprehension was so intense and overwhelming that she was on two medications: one for anxiety and depression and another for insomnia. She hadn't been able to sleep or relax for years, as it was so taxing to protect and monitor her fortune, and her health was in shambles.

She cried throughout the session and repeatedly asked me to reassure her—and even promise her—that her wealth would remain safe, which, of course, I couldn't do, at least not enough to ease her fears.

Clare was so attached to her material world and the need to control it that it consumed her. She had no joy, peace, or satisfaction. There was nothing I could do to relieve her pain, and she left more miserable than when she came because I couldn't guarantee her a sense of financial security.

Just as you should avoid clinging to things, it is also foolish to become overly attached to ideas or beliefs. What may work in one situation or circumstance may not serve in another. Some of the greatest suffering on the Earth plane at this time is centered on people's adherence to opposing beliefs and their attempts to impose their credos on others. This is happening on both personal and global levels. However, what is true for you may not be true for the person next to you, so arguing over these strongly held opinions is futile.

This does not make anyone wrong. You are individually and collectively in various stages of creative learning at all times. What feels correct for you in the moment may not necessarily seem that way for another, nor is it absolute Universal law. Part of your soul lesson on Earth is to find your personal truth, yet know that it is evolving and changing, not fixed, rigid, shared or unquestionable. There is no cosmic right or wrong; there is only love. If you are going to be attached to anything, let it be to this Divine quality—for yourself and others without condition. Release your unhealthy grasping for everything else.

Hold a belief as long as it produces the results you want. If these are no longer pleasing, surrender the position and choose another. You can discern if it has ceased to serve you by the experiences it is creating in your life.

A good friend of mine comes from a Polish Catholic background, and her family has struggled with a lack of money for several generations, something she felt especially keenly when she was very young. They survived on little, finding the resources they needed at secondhand stores and sharing clothes and beds—and everything else. This conditioned my friend to believe that wanting things, especially material objects, wasn't spiritually and morally okay. It certainly was a logical way to manage a large family with few resources and keep the frustration level down.

The notion of having a strong desire and using her creative spirit to go after it was discouraged as she was growing up, and she was rewarded for keeping her ambitions in check. But as an adult, her attachment to this scarcity consciousness has not helped her grow. For example, when faced with a cash shortfall, she chronically resolves to spend less rather than allow herself the joy of earning more.

Her fixation on self-denial shot down her visionary impulses, such as her idea of starting her own business. She dreamed for years of being a clothing designer and was a beautiful tailor. However, rather than taking the risk of striking out on her own, she told herself that she was too big for her britches and to shelve such grandiose thoughts. She perceived her attachment to lack as moral superiority, which made it especially difficult to change her attitude, but eventually she succeeded. She started tailoring for individuals, then opened a shop to sell her own creations. Now she's so busy that she's had to hire three other seamstresses to work for her. Once she let go of her old beliefs, the money started rolling in.

I, on the other hand, was raised in an environment where using our imaginative powers was central to our family's identity. If we needed something, we were expected to create it—and the sooner the better. This idea settled into me and took over, and I learned early in life to manifest things out of thin air.

I won TVs, contests, scholarships, and trips—even modeling jobs that gave me free clothes. I never rested. My attachment to nonstop accomplishment became a compulsion to keep going, dreaming, and doing, rarely stopping to rest or examine whether what I was pursuing was worth the effort.

I'm just now recognizing my need to let go of working so hard. My workaholism is just an unhealthy allegiance to an old belief that keeps me out of balance and prevents me from connecting with my authentic spirit. Unlike my friend, who believed that it's noble to do without, I was wedded to the idea that more is better. I'm now fully aware that neither position is true.

The Buddhist tradition is centered on nonattachment, but I've often sensed that Buddha really emphasized that not clinging to ideas is even more important than not grasping at things. I remember clearly that my metaphysical teacher Dr. Tully, with whom I studied spiritual law for many years, often quoted Shakespeare, saying, "Nothing is good or bad. Only thinking makes it so."

It is especially crucial that you detach from the need to win the regard of others. No one possesses the power to approve or disapprove of you. The Lord of the Universe created you, and all that God makes is good and holy—including you.

I read for an extremely gifted light worker, psychic, and healer who had the ability to use touch and prayer to reverse sickness in people's bodies and restore them to balance and wellness. It was extraordinary to be in her presence because her therapeutic vibration was so powerful, and I assured her that this work was her purpose.

Although she knew that she had a gift or "the touch," as she called it, she couldn't accept that this was her path because of the simple fact that she didn't have a degree in the field—never mind the fact that spiritual healing is not academically recognized (yet).

She was fixated on the idea that only a credential would give her permission to do her work legitimately, and she refused to believe otherwise. Furthermore, she was severely dyslexic and had barely made it through school, so if indeed there were a course that she could attend, she had such trouble reading that she probably wouldn't go.

Sadly, her stubborn adherence to her notion prevented her from using her talents, except to help a very few. She regularly turned people away out of fear that her service wasn't valid, and her beliefs kept her stuck and

*unfulfilled, doing temporary night jobs as a security guard. It all seemed
so silly to me, but then, who am I to be attached to her choices?*

To detach, simply let go. Imagine that you are holding something in your hand, then open it and let the object drop. To practice, take this exercise beyond imagination. Actually put something
in your palm, such as a spoon, eraser, or shoe, and hold on to it
as firmly as you possibly can. Then let go of it. Breaking free of
unhealthy grasping is nothing more than that, and is easy to do
once you decide to.

To detach does not mean to stop loving or caring; instead, you
no longer try to control so much and allow the Universe to direct
instead. Not doing this, paradoxically, can rob you of everything.

*I had a client named Alex who suffered many indignities growing
up in a broken, alcoholic home. He was shuttled among extended family
members, put in foster care, and eventually, at the age of 16, ended up
on the street. In addition, he did drugs, drank himself sick, dropped out
of school, and was involved in his own dysfunctional relationships.*

*Miraculously, through the grace of God, he finally sobered up. Regu-
larly attending 12-step programs, he even created a semblance of nor-
malcy and routine and started to live a calm existence. Yet due to his
trauma as a child and young man, he remained steadfastly attached to
two notions: 1) He came from losers and was a failure himself, and 2)
he could never trust anyone.*

*Living with these false ideas, he gradually withdrew from people and
shut them out. He worked as a driver for FedEx, lived alone, and became
more and more isolated. At 60, he died of a heart attack. It was three
days before anyone noticed that he was gone. He was sorely grieved by
his 12-step peers, who all expressed deep frustration at his refusal to let
go of his negative opinions and let them in to share his life.*

All suffering comes from attachment: "If only . . . he/she loved me . . . I had more money . . . I looked different . . . my family were another way . . . I had gone to school, I received more approval, or . . . I got what I wanted."

Detachment frees you from ego-centered fears and demands and reconnects you to your Higher Self. It is the antidote to your pain; and it allows you to flow with reality, gracefully and with peace of mind.

Now you can apply the lesson.

— If you constantly wish that you possessed more in life, have strong opinions about what is wrong with this world, judge others and yourself harshly, or are often extremely disappointed by others and life itself . . . then you are a **student** with regard to this lesson.

— If you cannot let go of past mistakes, worry excessively about what you have and do not have; try not to criticize, but do anyway; or take offense at the cards life has dealt you and think that things should be different but can still laugh about them . . . then you are an **apprentice.**

— If you are carefree and generous with all you have, believe in the motto "Easy come, easy go," do not sweat the small stuff, have your ethics and ideas but do not impose them on others or condemn those with different beliefs, or do not take life too seriously and are grateful for the little things . . . then you are a **journeyman.**

— If you rarely judge others and easily let things go; have experienced loss but do not dwell on it, preferring to just be happy; are thankful for all that you have and cannot believe that God has been so good to you; or feel prosperous, successful, and confident that your needs will always be met . . . then you are well on your way to **mastering** this lesson.

If You Are a **Student** . . .

- Start your day by counting your blessings.

- Give things away that you no longer need.

- Offer compliments, smiles, and appreciation if you feel you have nothing material to contribute.

- Pay attention to your attachments and notice how much pain they bring.

- Attend a funeral to help you remember what is important.

If You Are an **Apprentice** . . .

- Pick up a huge rock and carry it with you all day.

- See this object as representing your attachments and notice how heavy and burdensome it is.

- Make a list of the ideas that you are fixated on and tape it to the stone.

- When you are ready to lighten your load, let go and drop it.

If You Are a **Journeyman** . . .

- Every time you become annoyed, aggravated, or fearful, say "Detach" out loud and imagine dropping your irritation.

- Whenever you enter an argument, pause and ask yourself what you can let go of.

- Take a trapeze course, enroll in an aqua-massage class, or get a deep-tissue massage to release attachments that have settled in your physical body.

- Tithe or give away 10 percent of what you have.

If You Are on Your Way to **Mastering** this Lesson . . .

- Have preferences, not needs.

- Enjoy the peace of mind and relaxation that comes from being carefree and unfettered in life.

- Notice the pain that others suffer because of their attachments and be grateful that you have grown beyond this.

- Open your heart even more and let go of all past hurts, with appreciation for the gifts you received.

Your Soul's Lesson
Detach and Let Go

Your Soul's Purpose
To Travel Lightly Through Life

PART 11

Working with Divine Law

All Is in Divine Order

Everything that occurs on the human plane is in Divine Order at all times. No matter what unfolds, your soul has elected to experience it because of the opportunities it affords for growth. What you encounter on Earth reflects back to you both personally and collectively exactly what you have created based upon your focus and choices. The order or chaos you see on the outside, in the world, merely mirrors the harmony or discord that you choose on the inside. Spiritual Law ordains that for every thought, decision, and action that you outwardly express, you will experience the same energy returning to you.

Nothing is random, haphazard, or erratic. Every event is the consequence of some previous individual or group action on your part—whether in this life or in past ones, as the spiral of creativity continues from one incarnation to the next. God is not trying to teach you anything when life is difficult. The Creator only recognizes your Divinity. Instead, you are instructing *yourself* to become aware of your Sacred Essence, and you are learning this in the theater of human experience.

This lesson is challenging because what you undergo or observe at times hardly appears to have any logic or make sense at all. Nonetheless, Heavenly truth prevails. As spiritual, immortal beings, accept that—in spite of appearances—there *is* an unrelenting order to the Universe that you can trust.

In the end, you will all survive, learn, grow, heal, and reunite with your Creator. How this unfolds is determined by you. The way back to God is through the school of life, which you pass through as many times as you need to in order to learn. In spirit, you are timeless.

Recently, I spoke on the phone with a client who's a journalist in Austria. Reporting on the wars in the Balkans, Afghanistan, and Iraq has left her utterly demoralized. She's witnessed so much suffering over the years that she can't sleep at night. To be told that the Universe is operating perfectly after she'd seen families torn apart; children maimed by land mines; and men, women, and kids tortured by crazy people left her full of rage.

When I described the notion of Divine Order, she understood— or rather, misunderstood—the lesson to mean that the tragedies were ordained by God, or worse, that living beings deserved to experience such atrocities.

In fact, the Eternal Light does not condone barbarities or recognize death. In spite of appearances, the human spirit cannot be killed. No matter how sick or deranged your ego, or anyone else's becomes, or how destructive your choices are, on a soul level you are here to learn to use your creative powers correctly, and will eventually do so as you move from one lifetime to the next. Regardless of what occurs and what monstrous events may unfold, the Higher Self lives on and continues to grow. The only way to understand this is to directly come up against what your decisions manifest, including brutality.

The Universe operates according to impartial Spiritual Law. There is no one upstairs judging whether you are good boys and girls, ready to punish you at any given moment for your mistakes. On the contrary, God is only love, and you have been made in this Sacred Being's likeness as creators. What appears to happen to you randomly is actually what your soul *chooses* for your growth, no matter how painful, awful, or frightening it is. You learn through your experiences, and your progress is ultimately all that matters to your Core Self. The most important of all lessons is that there is no death.

The soul learns in spirals, not in direct, linear paths. Therefore, what you encounter today may have been initiated lifetimes ago and is only now coming to fruition. Furthermore, when you are in spirit between incarnations, you choose the direction of your learning. You may actually decide to undergo pain and suffering in order to understand something new. The path that you select may horrify your ego in present time, but it does serve your Higher Self. This is all part of Divine Order.

My Austrian client had been involved in war for several lifetimes in various roles—as a military leader, a rescuer, and a soldier. She'd experienced different aspects of battle, such as its power, the noble intentions of the combatants, and the righteousness of some conflicts in the past. In this time on Earth, her soul wanted to step back and objectively witness the destruction and pain. Although it was overwhelming to her, observing such relentless atrocities firsthand opened her heart and strengthened her resolve against war.

She hadn't had this awareness of her spiritual mission when she started her job. Yet from the beginning, her reporting went way beyond the facts. Her commentary served to educate people on an emotional level about the destructiveness of their choices. She was a powerful influence in helping others become conscious of their poor decisions. She was connected to her soul's purpose in communicating with people's feeling natures, while at the same time opening her own compassionate heart to others. Her path was in Divine Order, although her learning—as all growth can be at times—was extremely painful.

Step back from life occasionally and take in the grander view. Remember that you are spirit and that no matter how much you suffer in your human form, you are an empowered creator who does not and cannot die. The body comes and goes, and the emotions rise and fall. The mind struggles to keep control, but all of these activities are part of your temporary, physical existence. The more you identify with your limited ego, the more difficult it is to accept Divine Order. Only when you recall that you are an immortal spiritual being living in an impermanent body, and that you are here on the planet to experiment and learn to create responsibly, does anything make sense.

When you accept that you chart your course of experiences in order to further your soul's growth, life no longer seems so daunting, random, and scary. Instead, it transforms into intricate possibility. You begin to understand that Earth is a huge laboratory and that you are here dabbling in your creations. Some are glorious, while others are hideous. The marvelous experiments result in your victories and breakthroughs, and the awful ones lead to your tragedies. Every development teaches something and provides an opportunity to learn more.

Look past the physical, linear phenomena and the world of appearances in order to find the lessons of your life. Using your imagination, try to see from the perspective of your timeless soul that travels from one incarnation to the next, rather than from the view of your ego, which is trapped in fear.

I spoke recently with my client Jacqueline. At 45, she was distraught, overwhelmed, and extremely angry at life and God because her husband, Phil, had had a stroke four years earlier and was completely disabled. She challenged me by questioning, "How could this be in Divine Order? Phil ate well, exercised, ran every day, and was extremely committed to being physically fit. It just doesn't make sense. And what about me? Who will take care of me? He has to go to a nursing home because I can no longer take care of him, so what should I do? Sit by and watch as he remains nearly unconscious and unaware of me until he dies? Why did this happen to me? Where's the justice in this?"

I could understand her rage as she looked at the surface of her situation. But stepping back and taking in the larger view of their souls' journey together, I could immediately see how the Creator's Harmony was in play.

My psychic insight revealed that Jacqueline's husband had spent many past lives in military leadership roles, focusing on being invincible and invulnerable in every way—physically, mentally, and emotionally. Although he enjoyed great strength, strategic genius, and management ability, he hadn't embraced intimacy, emotional connection, or love during his soul's evolution.

His spirit chose to experience these things by giving up all control in this life and submitting to vulnerability and dependence. In light of his new goals, having a stroke was a highly creative way to achieve these soul intentions. As a consequence of his health problems, he was rendered completely helpless and totally reliant upon others. Although frightening for the ego and disheartening for his body, it was completely in alignment with his sacred plan.

Upon hearing this, Jacqueline even said that he'd somehow been amazingly resigned to his circumstances when he became disabled. In fact, he took it a lot better than she had.

As for her part in this situation, her past-life review revealed many incarnations as a nurse, nanny, caretaker, and wife—all traditional, supportive roles that annihilated her own identity and sense of independence. She'd been enslaved to others throughout her past; and in this sojourn on the planet, her soul had wanted to end such subservience and become a self-reliant, autonomous adult.

Her Divine Essence aligned with her husband's because his spiritual plan supported hers. His stroke gave her the opportunity to progress in her goals as well. She couldn't continue her self-sacrificing service to him—which was familiar but unfulfilling—because he was too disabled for her to care for him on her own. She also could no longer depend on him to support her, as he had catastrophic medical bills and no income. The situation forced her to become self-sufficient and emotionally strong in spite of her fears. Although from the ego's perspective, what had happened to them was horrific, on a soul level, it was in perfect alignment with their intentions to grow . . . which they did.

It wasn't possible to recognize or understand this with the analytical mind. The Divine Order in their life only became clear by observing through the eyes of the Higher Self and looking at the patterns of their previous incarnations.

Jacqueline admitted that when it happened, she immediately wondered if her husband's stroke was playing a part in her growth. In some measure, she knew that what I was saying was true. It's not that anyone "deserves" heartache so much as this challenge opened up doors that on a spiritual level they'd both sought to enter even though it was painful. That's how the spiritual sphere works.

Once you accept Divine Order, your Greater Consciousness begins to directly reveal to you your soul's plans and intentions.

Even if you do not intellectually or emotionally understand it as it unfolds, life will begin to make more sense.

My client Millie asked me how she could ever see the deeper order of existence as I can, especially when she was so emotionally distraught. In particular, she wanted to know why her teenage son, Brad, had died. Several years earlier, he'd been hit by a car and left to perish on the road-side near his house, with no witnesses to the accident. "What purpose is there to such a waste of life?" she asked.

My Higher Self revealed that Brad had exited under such mysterious and tragic conditions because in many past lives he'd run away from home in search of excitement and adventure—and to avoid responsibility. He was a chronic thrill seeker. In this incarnation, he wanted to be more responsible. It was his soul's desire to stop fleeing, stick with things, and learn about commitment and responsibility.

But these weren't easy lessons, and while he was alive, he seriously struggled with his intentions daily. In fact, on the night of his death, he wasn't merely taking a walk—he was falling into previous ego patterns and was secretly going away. His soul stopped him through death because it preferred to leave this world rather than continue again on the wrong course.

Millie was silent for a long time after I explained this. She said she'd fought constantly with her son when he was alive because he did run from responsibility and always seemed to seek the easy way out. In fact, he'd signed up for military service a month before his death and then regretted it. She suspected that he'd been escaping from that commitment the night of the accident.

Although she felt no better about Brad's death, something in what was revealed during our session resonated with her spirit. To answer her question about how to discover Divine Order in the face of chaos, all I could say was, "Believe it's there."

There is no way for you to understand your soul's plan on a mental level because the intellect is part of the ego, your temporary self. However, you will intuitively sense your spirit's direction when you trust the Greater Wisdom.

"So that's why at the age of 17, I inherited $5 million from an uncle I never knew?" my client Mark asked. "And does that mean that I don't have to feel guilty that I don't have to worry about money?"

"Yes," I replied. "Your soul has struggled for lifetimes with arduous work—even dying under extremely harsh conditions and waiting on others as a slave. For this stay on Earth, your spirit chose to receive in monetary terms the service and support you gave others in past incarnations. You simply cashed in."

"The funny thing is," he said, "although I'm financially comfortable, I'm not any happier than I was before. I'm less stressed but still lonely."

"That's an entirely different lesson," I explained. "Your Inner Being wanted to learn whether material wealth is the source of happiness. Now you're finding out the answer."

Do not judge events and experiences as good or bad according to your ego's point of view. Everything that happens is in Divine Order to support your soul's determination to grow.

My client Georgina was devastated when her first son was diagnosed with Down syndrome. A relatively young mother at the age of 30, she couldn't understand how this could have happened to her. My Higher Self revealed that in previous lives, her child had been a Buddhist monk whose soul was practicing detachment. He chose to be born without an ego as the ultimate challenge in this area. Down syndrome was the perfect path for him because people with this condition don't have a domineering will. Georgina had been his most devout student in the past and aligned with his spirit in this lifetime in order to learn complete release as well.

When she discovered his deeper Divine plan, a look of peace spread across her face. "This makes sense. I can do this with him," she said.

Years later, I met her again. She told me that her son was now a teenager with a job and a high school diploma. "He's my greatest joy," she said. "He taught me to see with my heart—not just my eyes. I'm so grateful that he allowed me to serve his beautiful soul once again."

The more you perceive every circumstance as grist for the mill of your spiritual growth, the more empowered you become. All circumstances turn into opportunities for your advancement. As you continue to accept Divine Order, the veil between past and present thins as your Higher Self reveals the perfect pattern hidden in all things.

Look at each aspect of your life through the filter of Divine Order, accepting that everything happens for a reason. It will allow you increased inner calm no matter what confusion surrounds you. Achieving personal peace is your greatest soul lesson and assures the highest level of creativity.

Now you can apply the lesson.

— If you think that the world has gone to hell in a handbasket and is filled with random chaos, are appalled and scared to death of the pain and horror on the planet, feel resentful and bitter you have been given such a bum deal, or are jealous of other people's luck and angry about the dark cloud over your head . . . then you are a **student** in learning this lesson.

— If you cannot believe that life is so crazy and wonder what is really going on, feel helpless at times but refuse to let problems get you down; become temporarily overwhelmed by circumstances but manage to rise above the turmoil in the end—and get creative once you recover; or want to believe that there is always a silver lining to every cloud, even when you cannot see it . . . then you are an **apprentice**.

— If you believe that what goes around comes around, look for the deeper meaning behind all events, focus on what you can learn when things do not go your way, or trust that the Universe is inherently good . . . then you are a **journeyman**.

— If you see life as a classroom and all events as soul lessons to learn from, refuse to feel like a victim no matter what occurs, have compassion for people suffering in painful world events and take personal steps to bring relief and comfort to others wherever you can, trust that there is Divine Order behind all things and strive to be responsible for your soul's growth, or choose to be peaceful regardless of what is happening around you . . . then you are well on your way to **mastering** this soul lesson.

If You Are a **Student** . . .

- Remember that you are a spiritual being—not just a physical body or ego-based intellect.

- Open your mind to the idea that all is in Divine Order and see what changes.

- Try to see or feel hidden connections behind all circumstances.

- Look at life with both your eyes and your heart.

If You Are an **Apprentice** . . .

- Notice areas in which you face recurring problems or patterns and consider what your soul would like to learn.

- Wonder about your past lives and ask your Higher Self to give you insight into what wisdom you can glean from previous incarnations.

- Make a list of situations in which silver linings did appear out of dark clouds.

- Trust that no matter what happens, your Inner Being has elected to have this experience in order to grow.

- Do not judge anything on surface value.

If You Are a **Journeyman** . . .

- List all the times that events ended up making sense in the long run.

- Ask your Greater Consciousness what you are supposed to learn in difficult situations, then listen to the answer.

- Be patient when life challenges you and trust that it is for a reason.

- Do not judge any situation as good or bad but realize that everything is a lesson that helps your soul grow.

If You Are on Your Way to **Mastering** this Lesson . . .

- Relax and enjoy things as they come.

- Confront present difficulties with peace and confidence in your heart that all is unfolding as it should.

- Be inspired by challenges, as they are opportunities to learn.

- Live and let live and go out and enjoy yourself.

Your Soul's Lesson
All Is in Divine Order

Your Soul's Purpose
To Trust in the Heavenly Plan

Reverse Your Perceptions

R everse your perceptions of security. In spite of what your emotions and intellect tell you, your safety and support are never controlled by anything or anyone other than your Creator. Only when you shift your awareness can you be truly free in your spirit.

Your ego plays tricks on you, enslaving you to appearances that feel real but, in fact, are not—or at least are not permanent. The Universe and all people and events are in constant motion and evolution. Nothing is fixed or immutable on the physical plane. It may seem so at the time, but at any moment, it can all change—and does.

All objects and conditions on Earth come into existence because of certain concentrated thoughts and beliefs. Therefore, if you want to alter a situation, accept what is so in present time, then simply reverse the focus and mind-set that created it. Do not dwell on the way things appear today if they are not what you want to experience. Instead, place your attention on the transformation that you desire. This does *not* call for denying today's reality, but means recognizing that the present circumstances are the result of long-held thought patterns. To manifest something else, choose different beliefs.

Reversal is the way to dis-create. This is an important tool to have since so many of your creations are not what you want. Knowing that you can undo things as readily as you generate them makes the classroom of life much more inviting.

I spoke with my client Larissa several years ago when she'd just ended a dreadful, sexless 12-year marriage to a withholding, emotionally shut-down man. During her reading, my Higher Self told her that she was now free "to become the star that [she] naturally was."

Shocked that I used those exact words, she said that she felt over-whelmingly guided to begin—at the age 46—a career in acting, print modeling, and voice-overs. With only a couple of months of professional training under her belt, she'd just gone on two professional auditions and had been called back for both within a few weeks. This was virtually unheard of in the entertainment industry, and she couldn't believe her luck. Yet at the same time, she also wasn't totally surprised because she felt so aligned with her decision. The casting calls were easy and fun for her.

In the next breath, however, she shifted gears and anxiously said that her ex-husband was fighting her to reduce his $4,000 in monthly child support to $1,800. She was panicked and told me that if he succeeded, she'd be totally poverty stricken. All her confidence in her burgeoning career went right out the window. Larissa felt that her work choice was right but that she couldn't count on it to bring in enough money to support her. She thought that she could only rely on her former partner's payments. That perception took away her freedom and made her completely dependent on him—the very thing she'd fought about with him when they were married and the reason she'd gotten divorced.

My Inner Wisdom guided her to engage the Law of Reversal. Although she was convinced that her ex-husband supported her and that only he could do so in the future, her belief wasn't accurate. She'd enslaved herself to him with her insecurity and lack of confidence, but she didn't actually need him to survive. I suggested that she reverse her dependence on him and place it where it belonged: squarely in the hands of her Higher Self and the Divine.

"Come on, Sonia," she said. "I believe in a higher power and all that, but I have two kids to feed and God won't do it."

I told her that she was wrong and that Infinite Spirit would not only support her dreams and responsibilities, but would, in fact, do so better than her ex-husband ever could, no matter what the legal system decided.

Larissa didn't believe me. She stayed focused on her perception and took her ex to court for continued child support. After eight months of *battling, she lost, getting even less than the $1,800 monthly payments he'd originally offered her. All the time that she was fighting him, she was letting her career flounder. She got many callbacks but few jobs.*

Panicked, she called me again, asking me if she should appeal the judge's decision, since without her ex-husband's support, she'd never make it.

Again I suggested that she reverse her attitude and depend on her Higher Self and God to take care of her. She said, "I'll have to now. I have no other choice."

"This is true," I affirmed, as I could tell she was clearly ready to learn Soul Lesson #13. She really didn't have any other option if she wanted to progress.

Faced with the reality of getting only $1,100 a month from her ex-husband, she began to place her security and support in Divine hands. Although she was motivated by fear, she was undeniably advancing. Three months into her new practice, Larissa called me a third time. She'd been cast in three well-paying national commercials and had just landed a small but regular role on a cable show.

Although she'd been forced into changing her attitude, she cooperated in the end. And in doing so, she finally gained the freedom from dependence that her spirit desired.

The Law of Reversal works even when you are afraid. We understand that it is no small feat to assure yourself that you are secure when bills stare you in the face, healthy when illness distracts you, or loved when it appears as though there is no one caring in your life. Do not deny what frightens you; simply do not dwell on it or become mesmerized or enslaved by it as though it were permanent.

My mother best summarized this law when she said, "Everything that you perceive to be true is so only as of now or yesterday. You haven't created tomorrow yet."

I just returned from Orlando, where I conducted a series of workshops on intuition and spiritual teachings. When I was sharing the power of Soul Lesson #13, a woman in the audience stood up and affirmed the power of reversal. She said that a year earlier, her daughter had been struggling with severe drug abuse, alcoholism, and ongoing depression. She was also involved in prostitution.

"Everything my senses reported back to me told me that I had lost her," said the mother, "but my spirit refused to agree with this perception. I wasn't in denial. I accepted her condition, but I wouldn't believe that she had no choice about it. Every time I spoke with her, thought about her, or heard others talk about her, I decided to affirm that her soul was changing and choosing health. I focused on her reversing her dependencies and connecting to her Creator for security instead of relying on drugs and other destructive habits.

"Although I was told by my family and even several doctors that I wasn't being realistic," she continued, "I chose to ignore them. I asked my Higher Self to speak to her soul and help her change her course. I wasn't afraid to do this because she said that she wanted a new life. It took five months, but the Law of Reversal worked. She voluntarily enrolled in a rehab program, moved back home, is seeing a physician for depression, and got back on track. Her spirit returned and redirected her."

Nothing in the Universe is immutable. By engaging your Divine Inner Intelligence, you can use the power of choice to shift situations. The more radical the change, the longer it may take to succeed. However, if you use the Law of Reversal consistently, you are guaranteed positive results sooner or later.

I observed this just last week when a beautiful, slender 35-year-old woman came up to me after a workshop and asked, "Remember me? I'm Debbie Lin from Denver."

When she said her name, my jaw dropped. The person I remembered was a morbidly obese teenager I knew years ago—not this gorgeous creature standing in front of me.

"Of course I do, but not like this," I answered, holding my hands out to her and admiring her loveliness.

"Thank goodness!" she exclaimed. "I couldn't stand the old me, and I finally got fed up. I decided to reverse the scale and set my intention to use my energy to shrink the numbers and my size."

"How did you do it?" I asked, wondering if she'd had gastric bypass surgery.

"I changed my idea about who I was becoming. Even though I was obese, I knew that my appearance didn't reflect who I was inside—a glamorous woman. I removed my attention from the external, fat me and placed it on my internal stunning self. The reversal changed me, including how I dressed, carried myself, and ate. I stopped bingeing out of self-loathing and began to choose foods in self-love. This led to even more new decisions, and eventually the incredible shrinking me emerged. I didn't diet per se. I just focused on who I wanted to be. The rest fell naturally into place."

The Law of Reversal works in all aspects of life and does not discriminate.

My client Pat struggled for years with paying her bills. She managed to make ends meet, but just barely, and there was little wiggle room for fun indulgences. After hearing me speak at a Unity church about the Law of Reversal, she decided to give it a try to help improve her finances.

She didn't deny the present reality of her monthly income and expenses, but she also realized that this was not a permanent situation. It could change. Shifting her dependency from her manager's job at a local supermarket and returning it to its rightful place with her Creator, she asked her Higher Self to become her boss and lead her to greater prosperity.

In order to solidify her reversal from financial struggle to abundance, she also decided to take up the practice of tithing, or giving away 10 percent of her income to her cause of choice. Although her ego screamed, "Are you crazy? You need that money to pay for gas, heat, and light!" she ignored it.

Her response to these fears was, "That may have been true yesterday, but today I'm creating more so that I have all that I need now and in the future."

A week after she began to tithe, she was promoted to general manager in her store, which included a $4,500 yearly raise. Three weeks after that, she inherited a three-story, six-unit apartment building from a favorite aunt in Baltimore who had passed on. It was paid in full and generated over $5,000 a month in rent. With these two changes, she was now flush with cash.

"I changed my ideas and stopped relying on others for security," Pat said. "The minute I put my faith in my Higher Self, everything started to flow again."

Perhaps the most important shift that you can make is to love others freely instead of withholding your heart. You get hurt because human nature can be harsh and ignorant as you collectively struggle to learn. But if you respond by cutting yourself off from compassion, you harm yourself even more.

I spoke with my client Denise, who'd decided long ago that she'd never again get in a love relationship after her first husband cheated on her with his secretary and left her to raise their small son alone. Bruised by that betrayal, she closed her heart and put up a virtual "go-away" sign for any would-be suitors to sense. She was unavailable and proudly said that there was no way she'd reverse her intention and suffer humiliation like that again.

True to her word, she never did let herself experience love again. She was cordial but distant, convinced that her choice gave her freedom. As time passed, however, that decision proved less than wise. Her son grew up and moved to the other side of the country. Brought up by someone with a closed heart, he'd become cold himself and didn't even think about the impact his actions had on his mother or anyone else.

Because Denise chose not to love, she also didn't cultivate any close friends, preserving her defenses and keeping others at bay. This all worked fine as she built up a design business, but when she was diagnosed with breast cancer and lymphoma in her late 50s, her self-imposed isolation no longer seemed to serve her.

Worse, even though she knew that she needed to change her behavior in order to address her disease in the best possible way, her pride wouldn't let her. When I saw her, the cancer was in its early stages. I gave her names, numbers, and numerous resources she could reach out to for help, and also encouraged her to reconnect with her son. All the while, she listened with her arms folded. I ultimately suggested that she reverse the decision she'd made about love all those years ago and have a change of heart.

She nodded as if considering it for a moment. Then she said, "Unless you have anything else to say, I guess I'll be going." I didn't have anything else to tell her, but I did give her a hug, which I felt she only partially accepted.

Less than two years later, I ran into a woman Denise had worked with and asked about her. This acquaintance said that my former client had died more than nine months earlier, alone. I felt so sad when I heard that—not so much about her death, but about her dying by herself. I accept that we all pass on, but to do so alone was a choice. I went to my favorite church that day and lit a candle for her spirit, wishing her more happiness as her soul journeyed on.

Every time you choose to love, your soul grows stronger and more connected to your true Source, God. Your Creator cares for you so much and has therefore given you the power of free will. The Law of Reversal simply suggests that you make decisions that do not trap or isolate you, or back you into a corner.

Again, do not confuse this soul lesson with denial. Acknowledge what is so, but remember that any creation in present time can be changed—maybe not immediately, but certainly, eventually. It takes time to manifest something and just as long to transform it.

Engage this tool when your senses overwhelm you and your brain tells you that what you see is a permanent reality: "I will always be fat," "I will always be broke," or "I will always be sick." This is not true. Shift your focus and you will reverse what you have drawn into your life.

To begin dis-creating now, write down the areas in which you have not generated ideal results—where you are disappointed or dissatisfied, or feel at the mercy of things outside of yourself. Recognize that each item you listed is only a creation or false perception that can and *wants* to be changed. In your mind's eye and emotional body, hold as clear a vision as possible of the reverse of the undesirable circumstance. Think about it, and feel and see it. This sets the transformation in motion.

You can practice the Law of Reversal by altering your behavior. Do things differently:

- Take a new way to work.

- Walk out the door backward.

- Shift your approach in an argument.

- Change your mind.

- Put your socks and shoes on before your other clothing.

- Relax your mental rigidity and let go of your resistance to transformation.

When you apply this law, you are no longer bound to anything other than that which always supports you—your loving Higher Self and Heavenly Creator.

Now you can apply the lesson.

— If you are closed minded and extremely righteous, refuse to listen to new ideas or views that oppose your own, see yourself or life in a certain fixed way, or do not understand how you can possibly alter the "truth" or reality . . . then you are a **student** with regard to this lesson.

— If you can see that changing a negative opinion might help but have yet to do it; cannot get past the idea that others (such as an employer, clients, family members, or friends) should pay your bills and take care of you; believe that positive thinking can only go so far; or dwell on things even though you know it is unhealthy . . . then you are an **apprentice.**

— If you reverse your thoughts as soon as you realize that they are not working; will not allow anything to keep you stuck; look for ways to exchange old ideas for different and better ones; or readily try new things . . . then you are a **journeyman.**

— If you do not let yourself wallow in unhappy conditions, are spontaneous and change in the moment, immediately walk away from the psychic sabotage of pessimism and victimhood in others, or begin each day by reviewing your creative direction and refocusing yourself before you get off base . . . then you are on your way to **mastering** this lesson.

If You Are a **Student** . . .

- Notice areas in which you are rigid and committed to negative perceptions or opinions.

- Make a list of what you want to reverse.

- Walk across a room, spell words, or get dressed backward, and free yourself from automatic behavior.

- Change one habit today.

If You Are an **Apprentice** . . .

- Seek out people who share your viewpoint about the direction in which you desire to go or the experience you want to create.

- Distance yourself from those whose beliefs reinforce detrimental conditions.

- Reverse your opinion or perception of at least one thing every day.

- Rearrange the furniture in your home.

If You Are a **Journeyman** . . .

- List what you do not want to continue to experience, and create a collage of what you wish to replace it with.

- Revamp one behavior a day. If you are normally shy, smile and say hello. If you usually act judgmental, refrain from making pronouncements. If you are habitually critical, be complimentary instead.

If You Are on Your Way to **Mastering** this Lesson . . .

- Reverse all ideas of external dependence and rely only on the Divine for everything.

- Change your withholding thoughts and love people more openly.

- Shift negative conversations by offering positive statements of gratitude.

- Continue to transform your identity by embracing the truth that you are spirit, dependent on and provided for by the Divine.

Your Soul's Lesson
Reverse Negative Creations

Your Soul's Purpose
To Dis-Create as Easily as You Create

Accept Death

Embrace what you fear most: that is, death. Stop associating your identity with your physical self and your present ego. These are only vehicles through which you travel on your earthly journey. You are not your body, your emotions, or your thoughts. You are Divine Immortal Spirit.

Throughout this entire soul curriculum, the fact that you are an Eternal Being is continually emphasized. And yet, even if you embrace this concept on an intellectual level, when it comes to death, you still become resistant and fearful, revealing how strong your attachment to your corporeal and emotional self really is. It is one thing to take mental refuge in the idea that you are an Everlasting Spirit; it is quite different to actually face the end of this life with peace and tranquility. Now is the time to learn.

Begin by noticing how prolific the cycle of death and rebirth is. You can see it everywhere, particularly in the natural world. Study a garden to observe how beginnings and endings are intertwined. Amidst the flowers, you will also glimpse decay. While some blossoms are bursting open, others are descending into rot. The most incredible part of this unfolding is that the dead vegetation is the best fuel for new growth. Each passing phase feeds the germination of the next cycle. This process is called the Wheel of Life and is evident in all things everywhere.

One of the greatest evolutionary steps that you can take as a soul is to fully release yourself from identifying with your earthly vehicle and accept your immortal spirit. When you do so, you no longer fear physical dissolution, and as a result, you stop allowing your ego to consume you with games contrived to avoid it. Accepting that one day your body will die allows you to live.

Those who have had a near-death experience affirm time and again that it was the most liberating juncture that they have ever come to, and ultimately their most joyful one.

My client James was a great lover of adventure, and he particularly loved riding motorcycles. He was constantly playing on the edge of safety, zooming up and down Lake Shore Drive in Chicago at three in the morning, sometimes driving up to 100 miles an hour.

In addition, he took cross-country rides, flying recklessly around mountain curves and through desert storms, and still couldn't get enough; he threw all caution to the wind. He never wore a helmet, rode at night when he couldn't see well, darted in and out of traffic as though playing cat and mouse, and always ignored speed limits.

I once accused him of having a death wish, and he laughed nervously in response. "Maybe," he said, "I never thought about it before."

The irony is that soon after this exchange, when traveling across western Nevada at a modest speed, just enjoying the day, a semitruck passed James and cut back in too closely, forcing him off the road. He fell 20 feet into a solid rock ditch, breaking nearly every bone, including his skull. He lay there for two days before someone noticed him and called an ambulance. He was airlifted out and spent the next four weeks in intensive care.

James later told me that he left his body after the accident. He saw himself lying on the ground, near death, crumpled, and bleeding, but he experienced absolutely no pain. Instead, he felt liberated from every hurt and anxiety he'd ever known. He realized in that peaceful state that his motorcycle adventures were just a way to escape from misery, worry, and loneliness—and yes, the fear of death. He was so scared of life and so consumed by his future demise that he threw himself into wild stunts to numb himself.

When he observed himself after the accident, he was completely detached and relieved of everything—a classic near-death experience. He realized that he hadn't lived his life; he'd only run from it. The minute he was back in his body, being airlifted out of the ditch, all the physical suffering came crashing in on him, but the deeper, more agonizing psychic pain was gone.

It took almost two years for James to physically heal from the accident, and he was left with a disfigured face and a noticeable limp. But he insists that the accident was the day he began to truly live. Having survived that ordeal with a consciousness not connected to his ego or his body gave him a sense of peace that nothing could disturb.

He subsequently gave up escapism and motorcycles. He fell in love with and became engaged to his physical therapist, and began speaking to people around the country about what had happened to him, teaching that there's life beyond this earthly experience.

James's story isn't unique. In America alone, there are almost two million documented cases of people who've had near-death experiences. I believe that the numbers are so high because there's a universal plan to accelerate our progress with respect to this particular lesson. It's easy to discount the stories of a handful of individuals, but it becomes much harder when hundreds of thousands talk about it.

I'm grateful to say that I've had two personal encounters with death that have given me a conscious experience of life beyond the body. The first was 25 years ago when, as a student in France, I developed appendicitis and a kidney infection. Not knowing what was going on and living alone, I lay down to get some relief, and the next thing I knew, I was in a hospital coming out of surgery. My landlady had checked on me after not seeing me come and go for three days. She found me delirious and rushed me to the emergency room.

While my body was being resuscitated and my appendix removed, I was in an altered reality, visiting with my deceased teacher Charlie, my Romanian grandmother, and several children who made me laugh. It was the most relaxed and happy I'd ever been in my life. I didn't want to leave their company as I found myself being quietly revived after surgery. I was in and out of consciousness for the next two days, all the while trying to get back to that blissful place. I was frustrated that I didn't succeed. But somehow, having been there, I also felt a deep sense of relief.

In my second near-death experience, I was riding in a car with my sister and niece when we were broadsided by another vehicle that ran a stop sign. The moment we were hit, I popped out of my body. I saw the two automobiles, my sister, my niece stuck in the back seat, and me smashed by the air bag . . . yet I felt free. Then I was back in my body, with my sister pulling me out of the car. I was reimmersed in the drama and commotion, feeling as though I were moving under water.

While I recuperated, I kept thinking about what had happened. What affected me most was how quiet and peaceful it had been in that pure spirit plane. Several days later, I realized that the reason it was so calm was that for a brief flash, I was free of my own thinking—my ego. That was the greatest aspect of temporarily being out of my physical self.

We all learn this lesson in our own way and time. Sometimes we realize through direct experience (as James and I did) that we're unlimited Eternal Beings. Occasionally, other souls teach us.

Death is only a gateway to another vibrational level of spiritual existence.

Recently at a workshop I was teaching in Kansas City, I met a woman whose four-year-old son had unexpectedly died a year earlier. She told me that on a Monday he'd told her, his father, and his brother that on Saturday he was going to heaven. He said that there were blue ponies and blue buildings there and that it was so beautiful that he could hardly wait to go.

Not being a particularly religious family or one to discuss the afterlife, they weren't sure what to make of this. Moreover, he was a perfectly healthy child and always had been, but his conversation about heaven kept up all week. On Friday, he suddenly developed a high temperature. Not too concerned, his parents gave him Tylenol and watched him a bit, but the fever didn't break.

On Saturday, they called his pediatrician, who advised them to go to the emergency room for further evaluation. Still not alarmed, they took him in. Evidently, an infection had set in overnight, and four hours after he was checked in, he died.

The family was devastated . . . but they couldn't deny that the boy himself had said that he was leaving and was eager to go.

This preview helped them deal with his death a little better. As hard as it was, it was difficult to feel so bad when their son had been so delighted to move on. My client said that she was still coming to terms with what had happened but was now consumed with using her experience to help other parents know that although their deceased children may no longer be physically present, their spirits live on. She was just sorting out how best to do that. I urged her to write about it, and that seemed to make sense.

Soon after, I met a woman at a Chicago workshop who'd had a similar experience. Her 24-year-old son had been perfectly healthy but not happy. The world demoralized him, and he said that he felt "dumbed down" by life on this planet and couldn't live in his true spirit. He announced to his family that he'd be leaving and that they shouldn't worry because he was looking forward to it. Not knowing what he meant, they thought he might be planning on moving. Instead, two weeks later, they found him unexpectedly dead of natural causes in his bedroom. He simply went to sleep and didn't wake up.

Again, the grief and pain, although overwhelming for the family, were tempered by the fact that he'd announced his own departure and been joyful, knowing that he was going away. His mother said, "I'm sad for me but glad for him."

On occasion, those beings who have passed on into spirit come back to help those of you who are most stuck; fear death; and cannot see, sense, or feel beyond the veil of the physical world. This is often deeply healing, comforting, and reassuring, and assists you in learning this most difficult soul lesson.

My client Betsy single-handedly raised her only son, Erwin, through high school, and was just about to send him off to join the Marines when his car got trapped on a railroad track the first day he drove it. He was hit and instantly killed by a train.

Bereaved beyond belief, she couldn't eat, sleep, or even speak, as she was so overwhelmed by her loss. This went on for two weeks, until one night, when she was half awake and half in a dream state, she saw Erwin in his graduation cap and gown, smiling broadly. He came very close and said, "Ma, stop crying. I graduated, and now I'm on my way."

He was so clear, radiant, and obviously happy with where he was that she could no longer weep.

"I realized," she said, "how convinced I was that being alive in this world was the best place to be. His visitation convinced me that there's something more. Having seen him, I now feel that he's okay and that he had completed his Earth journey, so I'm fine."

As hard as it was for Betsy to lose Erwin, she gained something as well. All her life, her son had been her only focus. After his death, she wrote a book and is now teaching and encouraging others to be grateful for life and do more than just endure.

"Erwin is with me," she said. "I feel his spirit everywhere I go, and it comforts and empowers me."

Physical mortality is a fact of life. However, everyone's spirit is eternal. Without this understanding, your days become a frightful game of overcome-the-odds and beat-the-clock. There is a big difference between only trying to avoid your demise and actually enjoying your existence. In attempting to escape dying, you resist living. You can free yourself from this scary illusion by noticing the cycle of death and rebirth in all things.

In my experience as a soul worker and teacher for more than 30 years, I've observed thousands of ways in which the Universe teaches us this lesson. Through sickness, accidents, suicide, old age, or natural causes, the physical body and ego pass away. It's never easy to accept, and it's always necessary to grieve over the loss, but it's unnatural when we don't address and seek to understand the ending of our lives as a normal part of our spirit's evolution.

Notice what is living or dying in your world right now. Physical death is only one aspect of this cycle. All things travel through the Wheel of Life. At all times, some are coming into existence, while others are fading away.

I see that wheel turning right now as my older daughter prepares to go to college. I find myself overwhelmed at times by how fast the years have flown, and I wonder where my baby, my child, and even my adolescent have gone. It makes me sad, and I question whether I've missed something or wasted the precious and now obviously limited time I've had her to myself on the wrong things.

And yet I'm also exhilarated about her flight into the world and excited to witness her confidence and enthusiasm. I tingle with anxiety as she gets ready to go. It's all good—both the passing of the old and the rising of the new.

I was again made aware of the cycle of living and dying last week after visiting my parents and celebrating my mother's 75th birthday. In my mind, my mom and dad, whom I love dearly, are forever young, so when I printed a photo I'd taken of them with my digital camera, I was shocked to see just how old they looked. I was seized at once with gratitude that they're both alive, in great health and spirits, and that I have such a wonderful connection with them.

But looking at their sweet, lined faces, I was also stricken with the consciousness that I won't always have them in this form, and I immediately wanted to return to Denver just to hug and kiss them once again while I still could.

Letting go of the physical self and ego liberates you from the restrictions of the earthly plane and frees you from limitation. As the body ages, it functions less efficiently. Just as you enjoy trading in your worn-out cars for new and better models, so your spirit likes moving on to fresh and more energetic vehicles.

Death also leads to new birth. The fallen leaves nourish the blooming flowers, and our previous and passing lives feed present and future generations. No matter how you maneuver to avoid this lesson, it, like all the others—if not more so—can only be learned by going through it.

"We think it's the worst thing to ever have to face," said one client of mine, who lost her husband in the World Trade Center on 9/11, "but miraculously, you get through it."

"It becomes easier," said another woman I did a reading for, a mother whose 23-year-old son was killed in Iraq, "when you accept that life keeps going and know that people's souls change forms but carry on. At least in understanding that, we can continue to connect with one another."

"It was my worst nightmare come true," said the young wife of a policeman who was shot and killed on the job. "But the very morning of his death, he said that he loved his life and felt so happy going to work. I know he died doing what he cared about."

Even as I write this, I'm looking out the window as the leaves on the catalpa tree in the front yard are dropping in the autumn cold. I'm listening to the workmen my husband, Patrick, has hired to repair our old porch as they curse at the rotting wood and cut it away. I can see my neighbor chasing after her new Labrador puppy, with her two-year-old daughter following behind.

The closer you look, the more you will see that there is no real separation between life and death. They just reflect different states of who you are, what you are shedding, and what you are becoming.

Although embracing the finite nature of the physical self is the most frightening of all soul lessons, in reality, it is the most liberating. When your main purpose is no longer to run from your eventual demise, but rather to make peace with it, you can actually begin to live fearlessly.

Now you can apply the lesson.

— If you cannot even think about death because it scares you so much; get depressed and sentimental every time you hear about someone passing away; refuse to talk about the subject and get angry when others do; or cry at the thought of losing people, even when they are alive and perfectly healthy . . . then you are a **student** in learning this lesson.

— If you accept that the body is temporary but grieve endlessly, think about ways to stay perpetually young and avoid dying, distract yourself from thoughts of the end of life by filling your days with crazy activities, or secretly harbor a death wish and therefore choose harmful behaviors . . . then you are an **apprentice**.

— If you are beginning to see beyond the physical and know that the spirit is immortal, wonder about past lives and even remember them, believe that the soul has completed a cycle when the body dies, appreciate the Wheel of Life without being overly sentimental, or look for new beginnings when things end . . . then you are a **journeyman.**

— If you have faced death and are no longer afraid; have an appreciation for the dissolution of all things and for fresh starts, welcoming them rather than clinging to the past; know that you have had previous lives and even remember them; or communicate comfortably with the spirit realm . . . then you are on the way to **mastering** this lesson.

If You Are a **Student** . . .

- Study nature and notice its cycles of life and death.

- Talk about your fear of physical mortality with a qualified spiritual counselor.

- Make a list of who and what has died in your life and how these endings have added to or affected your present existence.

- Talk to the spirits of those who have passed on and ask them to let you know that they are okay.

- Ask your Higher Self to remove your anxieties.

If You Are an **Apprentice** in this Lesson . . .

- Look for examples of where and how life prevails.

- Keep a journal regarding your feelings about death and the things in your world that are ready to die.

- Notice and discuss with others the cycles of your life that are coming to an end, the new ones that are beginning, and the good they bring.

- Spend time with those you cherish and take nothing for granted.

If You Are a **Journeyman** in this Lesson . . .

- Ask those you love who have passed on to connect with you in some way.

- Refer to yourself for the next week only as a Divine Being, using phrases, such as "My spirit says."

- Ask what in your life is trying to die or become infused with new energy.

- Talk openly with others about death, reincarnation, and your own past lives and theirs, until the conversation becomes comfortable.

If You Are on Your Way to **Mastering** this Lesson . . .

- Share any positive death or near-death experiences you have had with others.

- Keep a journal of any previous lives that you feel you have had.

- Pray to God, and ask your Higher Self to keep thinning the veil between this plane and the next, and to reveal your immortal nature to you.

Your Soul's Lesson
Accept Death

Your Soul's Purpose
To Live Without Fear

Embrace Life's Tests

Your soul progresses toward mastery by facing tests. These help you temper your human reactions and develop your higher spiritual ones. They appear in the form of challenges, disappointments, betrayals, upsets, trials, losses, and even injuries and sickness.

It is easy to believe that you are a Divine Immortal Soul when everything goes according to your wants and desires. It is more difficult to remember your Inner Being's purpose and power, and to remain connected to your Higher Self and centered, when life becomes demanding. It is only when you confront all situations with grace, patience, and love that you find your strength and ultimate freedom, and graduate to living in harmony with your Greater Consciousness.

Tests are not in place to harass you, but to move you toward soul mastery. They help you measure your spiritual understanding and mark your progress. In order to advance from one grade to the next in school, for example, you are given exams that you must pass. Similarly, to obtain a driver's license, your knowledge is evaluated, and you must demonstrate your competence on the road to ensure your safety, as well as that of others.

In these situations, the tests that you face are not intended to torment or hurt you; they are designed to make certain that there is nothing essential in the educational process that you have overlooked or misunderstood. They are there for your benefit, to assure your progress. For instance, if you lack the necessary knowledge of algebra, you will not have the tools to succeed in trigonometry and will therefore have to return to your studies and correct your weaknesses before moving on.

The same holds true for your sacred learning curve. As you move through the classroom of life, you encounter an endless stream of tests to expand your Inner Wisdom. Challenges do not arise to threaten you, although it certainly can feel that way when you are in the middle of one. These trials are only in place as a neutral aid to help ensure your spiritual progress and advance your purpose. You can then become aware of your soul's weaknesses and strengths and work to develop the areas that require further growth.

Just the other day, I read for my client Amy, who was facing a major Divine exam. A young mother at 24 with a nine-month-old and a two-year-old and a husband serving in the military in Iraq, she lost her home and everything they owned when Hurricane Katrina passed over the Mississippi Gulf Coast in August 2005.

Devastated, displaced, and alone, she was forced to go to her alcoholic parents' home in New Jersey for shelter. The day after she arrived, her mom and dad had a huge, explosive fight, and her mother kicked her father out of the house and asked for a divorce. Caught in a hurricane of another sort and too traumatized to deal with their troubles, Amy quickly packed up her children once again and sought refuge with her in-laws in Alabama.

Although they couldn't have been more loving toward her and the kids, her father-in-law had recently suffered a stroke and her mother-in-law had been diagnosed with ovarian cancer and was undergoing treatment. They had nothing to offer besides the roof over their heads, as they were barely surviving themselves.

When Amy called me, she was panicked, emotionally exhausted, and afraid. "Why is this happening to me?" she cried. "I'm not going to make it! Will this ever end?"

My guidance showed me quite a different perspective, which I invited her to consider.

"In spite of appearances, life isn't trying to do you in, Amy," I assured her. "You're just facing some stringent testing because you're so eager to grow your soul in this life. You've endured many losses, and I know that

they've been devastating, but what do you think might be behind all of this that could actually serve your spirit?" I asked, encouraging her to shift her focus from catastrophe to opportunity.

She was quiet for a time, then answered, "I've just faced my greatest fear of having nothing and no one to count on. Although I said that I can't take it, I'm finding that not only can I survive these hardships, I'm realizing just how tough I am. With no one to run to, I've had to turn inward, and surprisingly, I've found a well of strength I didn't know I had. Even though it's been difficult, I'm sure that I'm going to get through this."

"You see, Amy, you're passing a very difficult test," I said. "By confronting what you're most scared of on a soul level, you're finding—perhaps for the first time in your life—that you're strong and competent, especially if you rely on God to get you through this. You don't have to be afraid. You're handling it."

"You're right," she said. "It's just my habit to get so panicked and freak out. The truth is, I am coping with it all rather well, if I say so myself."

"Not only are you managing everything wonderfully," I continued, "but you're also succeeding in achieving your heart's secret desire to become a secure, confident woman at last. In the past two months, you've been forced by circumstances to take charge of your life and trust yourself. Although the process has been unbelievably hard, your accomplishment has been equally great. You've faced the worst losses and have come out stronger. And besides that, it only feels like you've lost everything when, in fact, you've just been given a chance by the Universe to create something better."

She said, "It's true. Because of these troubles, my husband's tour of duty was shortened and he gets to come home early. He told me that he's been stationed in San Diego, where we've always wanted to live, and we'll get help with housing once we arrive. In the big picture, it's worked out better than before."

No matter what happens, take it in stride and recognize it as part of the Divine curriculum for your soul's growth. When you are in the eye of life's storms, all things feel personal. With distance and objectivity, however, you begin to see more clearly how a challenge is just shaping your soul.

A difficult experience or episode is not an indication that you have somehow failed a test or deserve what you get. This notion is founded on the erroneous belief that there is a temperamental Almighty out there ready to punish you the minute you make mistakes. This is a remnant of patriarchal confusion and is not the truth.

God is love and only love, and you are always in the heart of it. The Creator never goes away or judges you—you abandon and criticize yourself. You play a child's game of hide-and-seek with God in believing that you can ever leave the Holy Presence when, in fact, you cannot. You are always surrounded and cherished by Infinite Spirit.

Your challenges in life are not Divine payback from a jealous Creator who does not like you or what you have done. They are simply indications that you are advancing along your soul's learning curve. You do not face difficulties as punishment; you attract them because you are moving to the next level of understanding of your sacred nature.

I read for a client last month who was more than ready to undertake some of her soul tests. A highly devoted woman who had belonged to a spiritual group with her husband for over 30 years, she meditated on a regular basis; volunteered at an abused women's shelter two days a week; and had taught children about dance, prayer, and meditation for more than 15 years.

Everyone who knew her agreed that she was nearly a saint in every way and marveled at her beautiful and loving essence. She, too, felt that she was on the right path and took inner satisfaction in the way she lived her life.

This held true until within a span of six months, her husband of 26 years left her for a younger member of their spiritual group, her son was arrested for attacking his wife and then sentenced to 18 months in jail, and she was diagnosed with stage I uterine cancer. That's when we met.

"Why is all of this happening to me?" she cried after she sat down in my office. "I've been good! I've been spiritual and selfless. What horrible things must I have done in the past to warrant so much pain and suffering?"

Sobbing hysterically, she continued, "Tell me, Sonia, was I a monster in a previous life? What else could explain why I deserve all this?"

Her question revealed a basic error in perception and one that secretly ruled all of her choices. She believed that what we get or what happens to us is based on how good or bad we've been.

The truth is that we're neither saints nor sinners. We're Divine children of God, holy and made of love. Our life's journey is designed by our soul to help us learn. The Creator assists us by agreeing to this curriculum and setting up tests for us to pass in order to progress.

As I do with all my clients, I explained that her suffering and challenges weren't payback for past sin, as she feared, but rather, were an opportunity given to her by God to grow even more. If she accepted it, she'd learn to stop living in fear, giving too much at her own expense, and being so hard on herself with her overly rigid spiritual practices.

Although she'd been married for decades and was devoted to her spouse and son, neither man was loving, kind, or appreciative of her, nor had they been for many years. Her husband had cheated on her many times over the years but had never left. Her grown son had frequently been physically abusive and demanding, and had even attacked her once or twice. Although her situation was painful to accept, she was being liberated from this bad treatment through recent events. God was inviting her to learn to love and honor herself the way she'd cherished and respected everyone else. Her cancer was in an early enough stage that she had a great chance of survival, and even complete remission.

None of what she faced was placed before her as punishment. Rather, her difficulties were given to her as an opportunity to quit beating up on herself and expand her capacity to love even more. She'd already mastered the soul lessons of unconditional care for others, as demonstrated by her relentless devotion and service to so many for so long.

She was now undergoing instruction in a new course on unlimited regard for <u>herself</u>. This was an even more challenging area of growth, as she was discovering, but in the end it would bring the greatest peace and reward.

Calmed and reassured that she didn't deserve this, as she'd feared at first, she smiled, then laughed. "Honestly," she confessed in sheer relief, "my first reaction to both my husband leaving and my son going to prison was 'Good riddance.' They were both as self-centered as they could be, and I don't miss them. I was more embarrassed by their behavior than anything else and thought it reflected poorly on me.

"And as for the cancer . . . even that spoke to me. Once I got over the shock, my first thought was, <u>At least now I have an excuse to take care of myself.</u> And perhaps because I've meditated for so long, my inner voice has assured me that I'll recover in the end. I know I'll get better—I just didn't want to disappoint God or feel like a bad girl. Now that I see all this as a test to advance my soul, I'm relieved. I must even admit that I'm better off all the way around because of it."

People embrace their challenges far more readily and turn to God for guidance and direction more quickly when a global crisis occurs than when facing more personal trials. This was evident after the 9/11 terrorist attacks in 2001, and again after the tsunami of December 2004. You all witnessed it again when the 2005 hurricanes swept across the Gulf states of the United States, and even during the major earthquake on October 8, 2005, in Pakistan.

You immediately recognized these catastrophes as great obstacles to overcome. You banded together in prayer and—at least to some degree—even worked together in love and service to heal these situations. You somehow intuitively knew that Divine forces were at work and humbly surrendered to higher wisdom.

These extreme events are often much easier to accept and embrace than minor ones because they evoke grand compassion and support. The world's heart swells and opens in great crises—at least temporarily—so you experience an expanse of love along with the hardships.

But soul tests are not always administered on a grand scale. In fact, what's often far more difficult are the small things—the daily slights, indignities, and irritants that you face. These situations are also spiritual exams that present you with an opportunity to expand your Inner Being.

My teacher Dr. Tully once suggested to me that each person is given no less than a dozen tests a day to grow the soul. It's up to us to recognize these opportunities in order to succeed with them.

For example, it's easy to be kind and loving to someone at a church or temple, or to be sweet and accepting to our friends at a party or social gathering—it's expected. But what do you do when no one's watching?

I once knew a spiritual therapist whom I greatly admired and felt was the epitome of grace and dignity. She was calm, patient, tolerant, and very wise, and I found her helpful during a very challenging period of my life. She was so good that I often referred my clients to her when they faced difficulties or needed guidance and support.

One person I referred to her was a young single mother with three little boys. Stressed and overwhelmed, she needed encouragement and motherly advice to see her through a particularly tough episode. She greatly respected this therapist as well, and began to see her on a weekly basis.

At one point last summer, my client called me, clearly upset. She'd been shopping with her sons earlier that day, and while she was putting her groceries in the trunk, another driver had backed into her vehicle, smashing her car's front end, and then sped off. She didn't get the perpetrator's license-plate number, but someone else in the parking lot did and gave it to her.

Distraught at the damage and having no money for repairs—not to mention being furious at the hit-and-run—she went to the police station and filled out a report. To her shock, she found out that the owner of the other automobile was her counselor. "So much for her calm, spiritual demeanor," she told me. "She had quite another side when no one was looking."

That error took a bigger toll on the therapist's reputation than her wallet. She had failed a soul test.

This isn't to suggest that we won't have our less-than-stellar moments. We all do. After all, part of being human is to be . . . well, human. We can get quite irritable, impatient, and rude sometimes. It's what we do with this energy that's the challenge.

You can never truly get away with less-than-loving behavior toward anyone—even yourself. Master teacher and great avatar Jesus Christ said it best: "Whatsoever you do to the least of my brothers, that you do unto me."

When you mistreat another, not only do you disrespect and hurt their Inner Being, you also harm and degrade your own. You may think that you can get away with this, especially if no one is looking, but you compromise your integrity and sacrifice your grace and dignity when you disparage someone else or are mean to yourself.

All humans have a shadow side—the thief, bully, petty tyrant, manipulator, and abuser, to name a few—especially when engaging with those whom you project to be greater or lesser than yourself. On a soul level, there is no hierarchy of importance: All spirits are equally precious. Any other perception is erroneous and keeps you limited. When you are tempted to judge another, recognize it as a well-placed test, given to you by your Higher Self as an opportunity to expand your awareness of the one shared Divine Spirit.

Your exam may come when you are being accosted by an intoxicated homeless man who lives out of a grocery cart and begs for money. Or it may emerge when you are cut off on the road by an arrogant young driver who impatiently rushes past. It may arise when you encounter a new salesperson who cannot answer your questions when you are running late; or it might arrive with a server who confuses your order not once but twice, and then overcharges you.

How do you face these soul tests? Are you patient, kind, and tolerant? Or are you impatient, abusive, and rude? It does not matter who observes this. You know the truth.

Each of these situations is placed in your path to give you a chance to exercise more love and tenderness. Some of these trials are easier to overcome than others. The more difficult something is, the more eager your soul is to grow to the next level. Accept all challenging moments with grace and dignity, knowing that they are tests and gifts from God.

I just spent four days at a gorgeous health resort in Tucson, Arizona, teaching this lesson to a class of 80 people. I emphasized in every way the need to practice unconditional love and to embrace every one of life's difficulties as an opportunity to grow the soul with ease, patience, and the knowledge that the Creator is working with us toward our mastery. It was easy enough to explain, and I spoke like a true expert. But the moment the course was over one afternoon, I was given the chance to walk my talk in front of several of my students.

The first challenge came when I went to the spa for my complimentary and well-deserved (as I believed) 80-minute mud wrap, which I'd been looking forward to for three months, ever since it had been offered as part of my compensation. When I arrived at the counter to check in, several participants in my course were present. To my surprise, the attendant told me that I had no appointment. Irritated but aware that I was being watched, I smiled and gently insisted that she look again.

She snapped that she'd already checked and that I was mistaken. I replied that I had a confirmation letter for the session.

"Go get it," she said curtly, "and let me see it."

I retrieved the note from my room, further aggravated that ten minutes of my treatment were now gone. She casually glanced at it, looked at her computer again, and then said, "That's a mistake. You still have no appointment," and turned her attention to the next client.

Aware that I was now being observed by at least ten of my students, I patiently asked, "So this means that I get no treatment?"

"Basically, yes," she answered, without a lick of remorse or concern for my feelings, and again went back to her work.

Staring in disbelief at her dismissal and thinking, <u>Don't you know who I am?</u> but knowing that I was under scrutiny, I quietly said, "So as the teacher of this large group, I'm out of luck?"

"Pretty much," she retorted, not even remotely interested in faking regret.

Wanting very much to blow up, I nevertheless refrained, knowing that I couldn't indulge my ego after telling my class to handle life with grace. Clearly, the Universe was having fun with me. I merely smiled and said, "Okay." I knew that this was my lesson for the day—God's delightful way of giving me the chance to practice what I preach.

Rather than being resistant, indignant, or fearful when faced with a tough situation, recognize it as an indication that your soul is ready to grow. Meet your challenges with courage and know that you are never given anything that you are not prepared for. Furthermore, you never have to undergo any test alone. Call on your guides, angelic helpers, and Higher Self to help you navigate through any difficulty that comes up. Ask for assistance and be open to receiving it, for it is available for you at any time.

Great and small trials will be laid in your path every day. Some you will pass, and others you will not—at least not the first time. Do not fret, because there will be more spiritual exams and opportunities to grow. They never stop. That is your reason for coming to the Earth plane. There is no better way to master your soul's purpose. It is not the tests that matter; it is the grace with which you accept and address them that is important.

Now you can apply the lesson.

— If you take every challenge or upset that you face personally, fear that you deserve what happens to you, only behave kindly when observed, let your shadow reign over your life, or are irritable and impatient much of the time . . . then you are a **student** in learning this lesson.

— If you overreact, panic, or get angry when undergoing difficulties; collapse in fear or act out in retaliation when things do not go your way; ask, "Why is this happening to me?" when the Universe throws you a curveball; or dwell on negative events way too long . . . then you are an **apprentice.**

— If you do not overinterpret events and respond calmly when situations go awry; see the correlation between what you preach and what you actually do and strive to keep them in harmony; behave with kindness even when there is no audience watching you; or recognize that it is not what happens but rather how you respond to what unfolds that matters . . . then you are a **journeyman.**

— If you see all events—whether good or bad—as God growing your spirit, look at every tough situation that arises as an indication that your soul has entered another learning curve, embrace difficulty calmly, or watch your emotions and keep them under control even when you are sorely tested . . . then you are on your way to **mastering** this lesson.

If You Are a **Student** . . .

- Step back and take a few deep breaths before reacting to an upset or challenge.

- Do not take anything that happens to you personally, even if it seems as though someone or something is out to get you.

- Think of any problems as tests.

- Remember that you are prepared for every spiritual exam that you face.

If You Are an **Apprentice** . . .

- Turn your life over to your Higher Self every morning and ask it to lead your day.

- Focus on remaining grounded and calm throughout any emotional, physical, or mental difficulty by using deep breathing, slow stretches, and prayer.

- Notice the silver lining in past hardships and look for the positive aspects of present challenges as well.

- Practice meditation and detachment on a daily basis so that when something burdensome occurs, you have experience in being calm.

If You Are a **Journeyman** . . .

- View challenges as an indication that your soul is growing.

- Look for the opportunity in every difficult situation or crisis.

- Ask God to guide you through every moment of every day with grace.

- Remind yourself that no matter how dark it may be in the moment, this too shall pass, as do all things in life.

If You Are on Your Way to **Mastering** this Lesson . . .

- Count the number of times in a day that you are tested as a spirit.

- Strive to pass each soul exam with more calm and grace than the one before.

- Pray to the Creator to give you the strength, clarity, patience, and love to continue facing challenges with dignity and strength.

- Expect and even look forward to tests, and let God know that you are willing and even excited to be tried, as it is a sign of your growth.

Your Soul's Lesson
The Soul Grows to Mastery Through Tests

Your Soul's Purpose
*To Respond to Life's Challenges with
Calm Acceptance, Creative Dignity, and Grace*

Temper Your Ego

Temper your ego and laugh at its demands. Surrender all sense of self-absorbed importance to God, and focus exclusively on living in your Divine Spirit. This will offer you permanent freedom from insecurity and a release from personal bondage.

This does not mean ridding yourself of your ego altogether, for it is not necessary to kill or suppress it. Your Creator gave it to you to help advance your soul's evolutionary course; and like a small, personal companion, when balanced it keeps you enthusiastic, motivated, and creative in expressing your spirit.

Just recognize the ego for what it is—a tool to work with—and teach it to serve you properly, rather than allowing it to block or override your Higher Self, as it so often tries to do. Keep it under control and do not let it intimidate you with its ridiculous demands and false perceptions.

Treat this part of yourself like a beloved pet that you have inherited. It is an undisciplined animal and can tear things up if given free rein, but with training and direction—and, of course, love and affection—it can be tempered and taught to act in the best interests of your soul.

Let your ego know that your Higher Self is in charge, and remind it daily that its assignment is to cherish and help your spirit—not the other way around. When your ego fulfills this positive role, it supports your growth. But if you do not harness and teach it to do so, life becomes an endless game of fear and survival, and this self-important aspect of yourself takes a beating, while subjecting you to one as well.

Reflect on all the painful things that your untempered ego puts you through. It kicks, screams, whines, gets wounded, becomes inflated, competes, and defends itself nonstop. Even if it is positively stroked, unless that is kept under control, it gets addicted and demanding and can never have enough praise. If you take a step back and observe this from the outside, you might begin to see how perpetually unsatisfied it is, never happy or at peace—at least not when depending on others or the exterior world for its sustenance.

I was recently reminded of how crazy my own ego can be and how miserable it can make me. I was asked to be the opening speaker at a very famous author's event in San Francisco. I couldn't believe my luck. To be in such esteemed company and to be allowed to address her crowd of 3,000 was quite an honor, and I was extremely flattered. I prepared for my talk for months. Not only did I practice what I wanted to say, but I got a new outfit and haircut to look my best.

When the big night came, I was ready. I shined in my 20 minutes before the audience and did such a good job that I even got a standing ovation. Floating on cloud nine, my ego couldn't have been happier or more full of itself.

After the event, the main speaker and I were escorted outside of the conference hall, where we were seated side-by-side at separate tables and asked to sign books. Still sailing on air, I readied my pen and prepared to receive my admiring fans—except that I didn't have any. Over 1,000 people lined up to see my far-more-famous colleague, but not a single soul waited to ask me for an autograph.

So much for my stellar moment! Not only was I ignored, but several participants smiled and waved from the other author's line, as though feeling sorry for me, and said, "I don't have one of your books now . . . maybe next time."

It was brutal, and my ego, which only moments earlier had been intoxicated with attention, now shriveled up and wanted to crawl under the table and hide. Unfortunately, I couldn't do that, and instead suffered through an hour of forcing myself to send pleasant looks to everyone as I sat alone.

Finally, the torture ended as my colleague was escorted away in her stretch limousine, and I was left by myself to walk the three blocks to my hotel. *The crowning insult came as I was crossing the street and one of the attendees honked her horn and yelled at me to get out of the way.*

By the time I got back to my room, my inner sense of pride was so confused that I didn't know whether to laugh or cry. Never before had I been so thoroughly applauded and then completely ignored in such a short period of time by the same crowd. It was ridiculous.

Thank God I saw that and started chuckling. How silly of me to get hooked into wanting such approval. I forgot that I do what I do because I love it, and not because I need applause. It was seductive, but the minute it disappeared, I felt as if I'd evaporated, too. The more I thought about it, the more I giggled at how comical I must have looked, sitting alone at my table. Thank heaven I remembered my spirit and how much I enjoy my work, whether I get accolades or not. The minute I reconnected to that, I was over my painful perceptions and back at peace. Living for approval, however briefly, was too devastating to continue. Acting from my Higher Self, however, brought me back to center.

Tempering the ego is a constant challenge because you want to feel good about what you do, and you love praise and recognition for a job well done. In fact, you relish compliments, no matter what you do. This is really not the problem. The trouble arises when you believe that you *need* such kudos to establish your worth, and worse, when you feel that you lose your value when you do not get positive strokes.

When you allow the opinions of others to define you, you give your power away and therefore set yourself up for failure—and even slavery. It is important to receive constructive feedback and even criticism if it is intended to strengthen your abilities; however, other people's views do not determine your merit. To believe otherwise is a grave error in judgment.

I have a Sicilian neighbor who's a prideful and meticulous electrician and painter. Some people who lived nearby hired him to rewire their home for central stereo several years ago, and he took the job very seriously. He carefully laid out the cables, wires, and speakers to ensure state-of-the-art sound, but he was obliged to maneuver around other workmen engaged in carpentry, drywall, and painting to renovate the house.

Because the electrician's standards were so high and he carried out his job alone, at times the other construction specialists were delayed as they were forced to accommodate him. Not surprisingly, they were frustrated and complained, causing the home owners to ask him to hurry.

My neighbor was mortally wounded by the criticism. How dare they tell him to speed up? He was a master craftsman doing the wiring for nearly nothing as a favor because these people were acquaintances, and instead of appreciating him, they insulted him to the core.

The crazy part of this (at least to me) is that the home owners were oblivious to how they'd devastated my friend. They had no idea that their comments insulted his pride, and wondered why he'd turned into such an enraged person.

Wanting to mind my own business, I said nothing. It wasn't my place to comment—but believe me, I wanted to. In the end, all of their bruised egos spiraled off into separate corners, and the friendship between them collapsed. Years later, both parties are still licking their wounds and intensely dislike each other, which is ridiculous from my noninvolved vantage point.

That is the destructive power of the overbearing and self-important part of yourself. It can and will take any situation that does not cater to it and use it as a reason to withhold love and friendship, alienate you from others, and cut you off from the flow of life.

The only way to avoid this is to keep this element in check and never take its perceptions seriously. Cherish it just as you would a new puppy, for example, but do not let it destroy you.

I have a client who's very ambitious about selling real estate and has made quite a nice living at it, as well as a name for herself. But rather than kick back and enjoy her wonderful (at least for her) profession, her ego never lets her rest. She starts her morning at 7 A.M. and works until midnight seven days a week. The minute she hears about another Realtor doing well, she takes it as a personal challenge and immediately sets about seducing his or her clients.

This woman is married but can't take a moment to relax with her husband for fear that she'll lose control of her business. Her ego is more addicted to being number one than to being happy. Every six months or so, she shows up at my office, richer every time, but also exhausted, anxious, and isolated. She's let her hubris run amok, and it's ruining her life. An untrained and unrestrained ego can do that. She's lost touch with her spirit and is now paranoid that everything she's built up will be taken from her.

I've tried to help her reconnect with her Higher Self, but she's under the spell of her pride. Eventually, her system will crash, and she'll return to her true self.

Allowing the ego to run your life will destroy you. It will never be satisfied, secure, or content. It does not matter what you accomplish, for it diminishes all your successes, and you immediately feel as though you are not good enough.

I know a highly successful musician who has sold millions of albums and won many international awards. An incredibly talented artist and songwriter, she should feel on top of the world, and does— until someone gives her a bad review or posts a negative comment on her Website. The harsh opinions of people she doesn't even know can wound her to the core.

The same holds true for a masterful writer friend of mine. The author of multiple bestsellers, a nasty comment from an interviewer or reviewer can send her reeling in pain and self-doubt.

To tame your ego, remember that you are created and loved by God, and perfect in the eyes of the Divine. Unless you are centered in your true identity as spirit, the wily part of your personality manipulates you endlessly. One of your greatest soul tests is to ignore it when it attempts to make you doubt yourself. The truth is, the problem is not so much the ego as the belief that you *are* this stubborn aspect of yourself. Love it and do not take it seriously when it becomes unreasonable. Also enjoy it as a tool, for it can be a delight and can make your life magical when it serves your Inner Being. When it tries to run you and becomes disconnected from your Source, say, "Stop," and then ask your Higher Self to take over.

To become free of its grip, lighten up and laugh at yourself often—and at any confusion, mistakes, and insecurities. The more you can have a sense of humor about your fragile ego, the more you will release yourself from its unhealthy power. Doing so will keep you connected to your Greater Consciousness and aligned with your purpose.

Now you can apply the lesson.

— If you are too insecure to laugh at anything; feel bound to other people's opinions and fear they do not like you; obsess and suffer over criticism; cannot accept compliments; judge yourself only by appearance, such as by your weight, height, skin, or hair . . . then you are a **student** with regard to this lesson.

— If you get stung by others' negative comments but do eventually recover; know when you are seeking approval and stop yourself; care about what people say about you but do not solicit their input; or occasionally tell stories that poke fun at yourself and have a good laugh . . . then you are an **apprentice**.

— If you feel good about yourself regardless of what you do, take criticism with a grain of salt, are able to chuckle at your mistakes and move on quickly, or are gentle and loving toward yourself and appreciative of your spirit . . . then you are a **journeyman**.

— If you love your personality but do not take it seriously; laugh easily at everything; do not berate or attack anyone, since you know that they are as Divine as you; or realize that life is a work in progress and enjoy how willing your ego is to get in the game and give it your best . . . then you are well on your way to **mastering** this lesson.

If You Are a **Student** . . .

- Look on the bright side of things and begin to take yourself less seriously.

- Avoid mirrors, scales, or any other means of harshly judging yourself.

- Refrain from criticizing others, because what goes around comes around.

- Focus on what is important, and ignore petty and trite comments and emotions.

If You Are an **Apprentice** . . .

- Forgive and forget negative feedback and slights from the past.

- Seek out comedy shows, movies, television, and books to help you remember to have a sense of humor about life.

- Host an "I'm wonderful" party, where everyone gets to brag about themselves freely and without repercussions.

- List your favorite talents, traits, qualities, and accomplishments, and admire the spirit behind your successes.

If You Are a **Journeyman** . . .

- When receiving criticism, accept what is accurate gratefully and without feeling defensive; let the rest of the comments go.

- Give yourself and others positive feedback and frequent appreciation.

- Say "Cancel" when someone attacks you—even if it is yourself.

- Tell on yourself—share past embarrassing moments with friends and laugh about things that you have heretofore kept hidden.

If You Are on Your Way to **Mastering** this Lesson . . .

- Enjoy your incredible, gorgeous spirit and let it shine.

- Take nothing personally, and remember that on some level we are all confused and all learning.

- Be kind to yourself and others.

- Laugh, laugh, and laugh some more.

Your Soul's Lesson
Treat Your Ego as a Beloved Pet

Your Soul's Purpose
To Laugh Your Way Through Life

Address Your Mistakes

Admit to and correct your mistakes. When you make ego-centered decisions, avoid responsibility, give your power away, bypass the work of growing your soul, and fail to love yourself, you will eventually be confronted by your errors until you repair them. This is Divine Law.

It may seem harsh or unfair to be held so accountable for everything in your life, but unless you are, you will never be fully in charge of your creative ability. Facing where you have gotten off track empowers you, for it is your chance to examine your choices and their outcomes, see where they fail to serve your growth, and make corrections.

Anytime you feel as though you are a victim, believe that you are unworthy, or are self-destructive or unloving to yourself or others, it is a sign that you have made an error somewhere along the way and need to alter your course to bring you back to center. Until you make the necessary changes, you will lose your power and fail to fulfill your purpose as a Divine Creative Being.

The Universe loves you and only holds you in pure adoration. It is not the one that is asking for corrections; it is your own soul that longs to come into alignment with the flow of Greater Consciousness.

Confront those areas where you have denied fault, exercised poor judgment, refused to grow, or given away your authority to others, and correct them as soon as they come to light. By admitting and addressing your mistakes as quickly as possible, you assume responsibility for your choices and take ownership of your strength and potential.

If you refuse to consciously admit your lapses in clear thinking or ignore your poor decisions indefinitely, sooner or later your soul will bring you face-to-face with these mistakes. Divine Law decrees that you must be completely responsible for all of your actions in life, for this is the only way to assure that you learn from them.

I had a wonderful and dear friend who had an unexpected encounter with her past errors, leaving her humbled and bedridden for over two months.

A devoted physical therapist, she gave every client who came to see her everything she could in order to serve their spirits, strengthen their souls, and relieve their bodies of stress. She took her time, often going way over schedule in order to give them her best efforts. She worked on weekends, evenings, and even holidays if necessary, never turning away a patient. She did this for years, feeling good about herself and her ability to help others.

Then one day, out of the blue, she woke up with tremendous lower-back pain. Not sure what was wrong, she rushed to the emergency room, where she was x-rayed for everything from kidney stones to sciatica, but received no conclusive diagnosis. No one could determine the cause of her suffering. Sent home with painkillers and told to rest, she determined that it was just a pulled muscle and gave it no more thought.

However, the agony increased, traveled from her back to her legs and shoulders, and was so severe that she nearly lost her mind. She went back to the doctor, had an MRI, and saw nerve specialists and a massage therapist, but found no relief. If anything, her torment became worse. She tried acupuncture, stretching, walking, hot tubs, and even Chinese cupping to no avail.

After two weeks, a rash broke out on her back, and finally, it was determined that she had shingles. The diagnosis brought only partial relief, because there's no cure for this malady. She had to ride it out for six more weeks before it began to subside. The entire episode left her depleted, exhausted, and broke.

As I spoke with her one afternoon, she was sobbing in pain and said, "I know that I brought this on myself. Although I adore my work, I pushed myself way past the loving point and worked out of duty and the fear of saying no. I doled out tender care to everyone else's body while disrespecting my own—and I did it for a long, long time. This is my reckoning. My physical self finally rebelled or collapsed or both. When I get over this, I'm going to do things a lot differently."

Your soul does not step in to help you change until it becomes clear that left to your ego's devices, you will continue to make the same mistakes. Course corrections are spiritual interventions. They occur when you live in constant denial or ignore your errors rather than being honest and confronting them. Although such a mediation can be painful, it is your saving grace in the end.

I had a client who continually aligned herself with less-than-savory male companions. A registered nurse who put in long, hard hours at the county hospital, she kept falling in love with her patients, even though most were small-time (and some not-so-small-time) criminals. She took them in after they were released from medical supervision, paid their way, gave them a place to live, and sometimes even provided them with drugs she stole from work. Feeling sorry for these men and convincing herself that she was a good Samaritan, she was ripped off and abused every time. Worse, she sacrificed her integrity by stealing, disrespecting herself, and aiding and abetting illegal behavior. She couldn't admit that she had such low self-esteem that she was seducing them just so she wouldn't be alone.

Her day of reckoning came when she pilfered some Valium to give to her then live-in boyfriend and was caught. She not only lost her job, but also her nurse's license, and was prosecuted for stealing controlled substances. Past thefts were uncovered, and she was sentenced to six months in jail. Horrified that she was now a convicted criminal herself, she couldn't believe her fate. And yet, once she served her time, she confessed that it was the best thing that had ever happened to her.

Behind bars, she sobered up emotionally. She joined a therapy group and got the help she'd refused to admit she needed. As humiliated and painful as her losses and incarceration were, she was still better off than before. She was forced to stop setting herself up to be abused by men and bartering her integrity for "love." She used the gardening skills she acquired while serving her sentence to start a new career in landscaping. She was finally being true to her spirit, and in the end, her difficult experience was worth it.

The Universe flows with the energy of truth, love, and integrity at all times. Anything that moves away from these qualities is eventually redirected. All choices will ultimately be reconciled with higher truth.

In the long run, course corrections make life more fulfilling because they align you with your Divine Self and purpose. They are not put in place to harm you, but to keep you from hurting yourself.

My client Joshua had every material possession a person could hope for. He was born into a wealthy family, was handsome, and made a fortune in real estate. He had million-dollar homes in six states, was in great demand on the dating circuit, and traveled all over the world. The problem with Joshua was that he chose to live only on a superficial level. He kept his feelings to himself, never got too close to anyone, went out with a woman only for only a short while before moving on to the next, and was noncommittal and artificial. He wore a constant smile and never let himself depend on anyone.

This worked well for him until he was 57, when everything changed suddenly. The stock market collapsed, and he lost several investment properties. His business partner of 20 years embezzled more than $15 million and left the country. His two sisters were diagnosed with cancer in the same month, and as he was driving to Georgia to see them, he broke both legs in an accident.

His secure, independent world fell apart. He had no friends to turn to, and his only family, his sisters, were too sick to help. He lost more than half his fortune and was faced with the likelihood that he would walk with a serious limp and probably never play sports again. His superficial life was over.

Joshua's lesson became apparent: He needed to open his heart and connect with people in a deeper, more meaningful way, which he'd refused to do until then. He learned slowly. He moved to Georgia to be with his siblings, and after undergoing a year of physical therapy, he regained the ability to walk. He reorganized his business and started to forge better working relationships. He also joined the Unity church and became involved in charitable endeavors. He stopped dating casually and reconnected with a high school girlfriend, someone he'd actually felt love for long ago.

The climb to stability has been hard, but he's doing it. Most important, he's finally admitted that he needs people and has stopped controlling and using others with his money. He no longer believes that his wealth makes him superior. In short, Joshua's losses humbled him and opened his heart.

You will eventually confront every mistake you have ever made.

When I think of my own misfortunes in life, I, too, can see the higher forces of the Universe at work, keeping me on my path and true to my Spirit.

Years ago I became an airline attendant for all the wrong reasons. I wanted to escape a claustrophobic relationship with a man, get out of Denver, and see the world. I also longed for more glamour. However, I didn't want to do the actual work—I just wanted the benefits.

Weeks after I was hired, I developed a severe case of sciatica and could barely walk. Amazingly, I made it through training. I was based in Chicago, away from my stagnant relationship—or so I thought. (He followed me three months later.) To make matters worse, my flights were always to the least exciting cities: Cincinnati, Peoria, and Omaha. (No offense to those cities, but they were hardly an adventure.)

I was sick, smothered, and trapped by the job. I didn't quit, although I should have because I was miserable. My liberation didn't come for five more years when the attendants went on strike. I was elated, and it took that event to jar me loose. When it ended and we were all called back, I decided that I'd had enough unhappiness and didn't return. Instead, I committed to my spiritual path and to what I'm doing today.

The severe Earth changes that you have been witnessing are course corrections on a global level. The planet itself is a living, breathing, conscious being that is no longer willing to allow your thoughtless or intentional disrespect to continue. This is why she is unleashing tsunamis and record-breaking numbers of hurricanes and earthquakes that wipe out miles and miles of land and thousands of people. She is bringing to your attention your collective hubris, especially with regard to your lack of reverence and care for the natural world.

Look for evidence of soul interventions in your life today. Where are you being confronted by past mistakes? Where have you failed to be honest, keep your word, stay true to yourself, or love yourself? And what has it cost you? It does not even have to be catastrophic, for reckoning comes in subtle ways, too.

My husband and I just had a painful experience of course corrections with the upkeep of our old Victorian home in Chicago. We knew when we bought it that it would require constant attention, especially to the exterior. Still, we ignored our duties and did virtually nothing to the outside for eight years. We finally noticed the paint flaking away and agreed that it was time to give it a fresh coat.

Once the work began, we were informed that we'd have to do a lot more than just slap on some fresh color. Due to our neglect, the wood had rotted in several places, requiring repair before painting would be possible. By the time everything was completed, it cost us a small fortune. Although shocked by the price, we both knew that we had only our neglect to blame. It was a steep penalty to pay, but rest assured that it will never happen again—we're too angry to let it.

At first, it can feel quite overwhelming to be highly accountable, yet this leads you to soul mastery. Your ego resists being fully responsible for your choices. It prefers to blame others, remain a victim, and stay in a vicious cycle of powerlessness. But the Universe never sees you as helpless because you are not.

I remember just a few months back getting my beloved blue VW bug completely repaired—bumper to bumper. I had every dent, scratch, and flaw fixed, and restored the exterior to nearly brand new. Driving home, I vowed that this was going to be my special car, and now that it was in stellar condition, only I was going to drive it—not my husband or two teenage daughters.

Three weeks later, my daughter Sabrina rushed into my office and insisted that I let her use the Beetle to get to a forgotten appointment. Unwilling to refuse, as I was engaged with a client and didn't want to deal with Sabrina's reaction, I handed over the keys.

An hour later, I received a hysterical phone call from her. Someone *had rear-ended her at a stoplight, smashed in the trunk, then sped off. My car was trashed. To make matters worse, not only could Sabrina not understand why I was upset, she was infuriated that I wasn't more concerned about her well-being. Perhaps I should have been, but all I could think of was that the incident served me right. I'd been too wimpy and acquiescent about my decision and gave in without any resistance. Another $2,000 in repairs taught me a lesson—not to say yes when I mean no.*

In spite of the short-term pain that often comes with facing your mistakes, you immediately experience the soul benefits of doing so. When you align with your spirit, you free the power of the Universe to flow through you. When you cooperate with Divine Law and fully commit to living in truth, something miraculous happens: Drama subsides and life begins to unfold peacefully. This is the natural way and in order with the Sacred Plan.

Become the master of your experience rather than a victim by addressing your errors as soon as you become aware of them. Although it may be challenging, humbling, and disruptive to admit that you have had a lapse in judgment, it is always empowering on a soul level.

When things do not go your way, allow at least one part of you to step back and observe without reacting. Ask yourself, "What can I learn from this? What am I ignoring, denying, fearing, or tolerating that is not in alignment with my Higher Self?"

Do not blame yourself, but rather seek to understand where you've gone astray in your choices. Once you face your mistakes and set about correcting them, you gain a freedom that nothing can take away.

As Shakespeare so eloquently said, "To thine own self be true."

Now you can apply this lesson.

— If you are extremely defensive, refuse to see the connection between the misery in your life and your actions and decisions, lie when you make a mistake, or blame others for your errors . . . then you are a **student** in learning this lesson.

— If you have no idea why bad things happen but are willing to make the best of situations; tend to second-guess yourself and follow other people's counsel instead of your own, only to regret it later; make decisions that you know are not good for you; or easily get thrown off your path by others, even when you do not want to be . . . then you are an **apprentice.**

— If you dislike it when problems develop, but look in the mirror first to figure out your role in them; admit mistakes readily without hanging on to guilt; examine your choices as soon as something goes awry; or often reflect on your actions to be certain you are being true to your spirit . . . then you are a **journeyman.**

— If you experience less and less drama in your life, make course corrections on your own before difficulties arise, address uncomfortable situations quickly rather than avoiding them, or move beyond personal dilemmas and seek to right imbalances in the environment and contribute to solving other social issues . . . then you are on your way to **mastering** this lesson.

If You Are a **Student** . . .

- Admit what you are denying or refusing to take responsibility for.

- Make a list of your troubles and see if you can make any connection between your choices and your problems.

- List the poor decisions you have made and what you are willing to do to change them.

- Think through your options before you act.

If You Are an **Apprentice** . . .

- Slow down and pay attention to signals, information, or indications that things are out of balance.

- Do not ignore the small tasks that need to be taken care of.

- Do not put off till tomorrow or next week what needs attention now.

- If something feels wrong or does not ring true, speak up, talk it over, and make a final decision that sits well in your heart.

If You Are a **Journeyman** . . .

- Take a stand for what feels right, even if it is uncomfortable.

- Follow your inner prompting, even if it is the unpopular thing to do.

- Never blame another. Look for solutions instead.

- Notice what is weak in your life or character and ask for outside help to strengthen it.

If You Are on Your Way to **Mastering** this Lesson . . .

- Ask yourself where you are not growing, and focus on developing that area.

- Enjoy the calm and quiet that you are creating.

- Analyze all aspects of your life, including your physical health, and notice what needs reinforcement.

- When crises arise, step back and pause before reacting.

- Take your time when making decisions, allowing yourself the opportunity to check in with your Higher Self first.

Your Soul's Lesson
Address Your Mistakes

Your Soul's Purpose
To Live with Integrity in All Areas of Your Life

Actively Meditate

A ctively meditate. This is the most effective way to shape your
world as you wish. The laws of the Universe dictate that you
create what you focus on. You do not manifest that which merely
flies through your mind, but rather what you concentrate on.

Meditation is the practice of disciplined thought. Holding an
intense idea over a long period of time brings about its counterpart
in the physical world. Quantum physics verifies that your experiences are simply thought in motion. That is why contemplation is
so powerful: It literally molds and generates everything that you
encounter.

The secret is to meditate actively rather than passively. Let us
begin by defining the latter method, which is the most common
model in your world, and suggests a rigid and narrow discipline
that calls for sitting still and emptying the mind of all thought
for an extended period of time. This technique is part of an age of
consciousness that is ending. Although it is certainly one option, it
is by no means the only approach, and it is not the most productive
one in the present era of creation.

There is a more powerful form called *active meditation* that can
assist you even further. In this practice, you hold your unwavering
attention on something specific that you wish to experience. Seriously focusing on a single thought will bring it into manifestation
every time.

Unswerving concentration literally shapes the psychic fluid
of the physical world according to your thought. Sitting passively
and centering your mind on nothing therefore becomes a waste

of time. Resting quietly, however, and actively musing on the love of God and the Divine Spirit in all living things is quite another matter. Just imagine what your life experience would be like if you directed all your attention to how much the Almighty cares for you and to how much joy the Lord of the Universe takes in showering you with blessings.

My student Ed decided to do just that when I proposed the idea. He reported later that it was far easier said than done. Once he began, his first insight was that he was extremely focused on how little love he felt and noticed in his life. Meditating on how much the Creator loved him consequently took some effort.

He decided to support his new endeavor by looking for evidence of God's love. He first found it in the beauty of his garden, which brought him tremendous joy when it bloomed. He realized that it was a sacred gift to him. He also saw clear indications of Divine adoration in his good health. At the age of 52, while many of his friends and family members struggled with myriad medical problems, he suffered from none. In addition, he became aware of how he was cherished by his Creator in his job as a surveyor, which he truly enjoyed. It gave him plenty of freedom, a variety of work, and paid sufficient income.

Starting with these realizations, Ed began to concentrate his full attention on the many other ways in which God loved him and became open to discovering new things. The first major shift in his life occurred two months later. Suddenly, women everywhere started to ask him out on dates, which had never happened before. After all, he was over 50, short, and balding, with a good-sized paunch and thick eyeglasses. But they were still interested and invited him out—sometimes twice in a day. They were all beautiful as well.

Encouraged by this agreeable development, he doubled his meditation time and even took it to a verbal level. He decided that his mantra would be a statement of just how much God cared for him and how grateful he was for that. By the fourth month, while steadily dating a very attractive woman whom he liked very much, he was contacted by two headhunters who wanted to recruit him for better-paying, more attractive positions than the one he presently held. Not wanting to be unfair to his employer, he told his boss about the offer, which he matched. As a result, Ed kept his job and got a raise that he hadn't even been seeking.

Continuing his experiment, he expanded his contemplative practice, choosing now to focus on being kind and loving to everyone he met. After several months, he noticed that his cynical, dark sense of humor—a long-held defensive shield—had evaporated. Or rather, his sister observed the change and pointed it out to him. She remarked how much more pleasant he'd become and how she and the rest of the family looked forward to seeing him these days. He was genuinely fun to be around and didn't upset them with his sarcasm anymore.

About a year passed before we next spoke. "I never would have believed that I'd call myself a meditator," he said, "but your theory captured my imagination. Focusing on being loved has given me just about everything missing in my life, except for maybe some more hair." At this, he chuckled and patted his bald pate.

That night, he called me, laughing hysterically. "Guess what?!" he exclaimed. "I was just contacted by a medical group looking for volunteers for hair-growth research. Someone recommended me to them. If I want to, I can get two years' worth of stimulation treatments for free. Now that's truly love from God!"

Do not fear the practice of meditation or allow it to intimidate you. You may believe that you cannot concentrate or be scared that you will do it incorrectly, but in reality, you do it all the time and are quite masterful at it. However, you call it something else: *worry.* Anxiety is an intensely active contemplation because it focuses your attention on one thing to the exclusion of all else. Just ask any group of people at any given time what they are thinking about, and seven out of ten will tell you that it is something they are stewing over.

I had a wealthy client named Joe who constantly dwelled on getting taken advantage of by beautiful younger women who were only interested in him for his fortune. So obsessed was he with this meditation that no adult female was beyond suspicion. Sure enough, his theory proved accurate, as each lady he went out with inevitably fell into financial misfortune within weeks of meeting him and asked him for money—all except two, Maria and Sylvia, who had plenty of their own. Neither one of them, however, was of much interest to Joe beyond one or two dates. He said that they weren't attractive and lacked the chemistry he was looking for. This "chemistry," I believe, was the experience he focused on, which was going out with cash-strapped, dependent younger women.

Joe's situation isn't exceptional. We all continually meditate on our expectations, only we often don't realize how powerful this is.

For variety, and to engage your creative faculties in this process, imagine that you are going fishing in the Divine Sea of Possibility. Visualize your consciousness as an energetic question mark that forms a fishing hook, and cast it into the waters. Remain focused and patient, and in time, your meditative tool will draw your desired experience to you.

I grew up in Colorado and remember going fishing as a very young and excited child with my mom at Lake Evans in the mountains outside of Denver. I liked this sport because it was an adventure, so this view of contemplation immediately captured my imagination and took hold.

As soon as the Emissaries of the Third Ray suggested it, I started casting my meditative hook for little things, such as inspiration in my readings with clients, help when I taught workshops, and direction in my relationships. Eventually, I began to seek ideas for books, essays, guided visualizations for students, and ways to improve the quality of my family life. The more I fished, the more insights I "caught," and soon the process became automatic. Now I go to the Divine Sea of Possibility for everything I need.

So far, this is working brilliantly for me; I've snagged things that are far more gorgeous than I could have ever devised on my own. This is a wonderful method for anyone stuck in a rut or feeling uninspired.

Active "fishing" is a most entertaining form of contemplation. It also bypasses your ego's limited perceptions and gives you immediate access to Divine solutions.

It is important when doing this to be patient, because the greatest obstacle to any form of meditation is a short attention span. Just as surely as you will not catch fish if you throw a line into the sea and then immediately pull it out, your meditative hook will not yield results if you are antsy and do not allow it to remain still.

Television and the media have shortened the length of time you can focus, and conditioned you to expect instant gratification. This is unrealistic, since the vibration of the physical plane moves at its own rhythm and pace. If you are unhurried and consistent when you meditate, the Universe will ultimately manifest your desires according to its own timetable. That is Divine Law.

Fishing for solutions makes meditation an exciting, blessed, and creative adventure.

Many great inventors—including Thomas Edison, Albert Einstein, the Wright brothers, Walt Disney, Marie Curie, and Louis Pasteur—cite a similar form of concentration as the means by which they discovered their secrets. They all constantly meditated while searching for insights, creations, and solutions, and focused on reeling in answers and inspiration. It's not uncommon even now to hear an innovative person—or anyone, for that matter—say that a thought "grabbed hold of them" or that they got "hooked" on an idea.

I experienced this myself when I started concentrating last summer on how wonderful it would be to spend a week in Aspen with my family over Christmas. I began to research the idea, only to find that it was formidably expensive. Undeterred, I simply meditated on my desire and considered how I might hook it into becoming possible. The key was that I <u>wondered</u>—I didn't worry, nor did I try to figure it out. I just cast my mind into the Sea of Possibility and waited for something to bite. Six weeks later, I attended a fund-raiser for a health-care clinic in Kansas City, and the grand prize in one of their contests was seven days in a three-bedroom home in Aspen.

<u>Aha!</u> I thought. <u>This is what I hooked!</u> To my not-very-surprised delight, I won. I called to see if I could use the house over Christmas, and was told that that was the only week when it was booked by the owners. Tremendously disappointed, I said that I understood. After all, it was one of the most desirable winter-vacation spots in the world during the most popular week of the year. However, I kept concentrating on attracting my special holiday. I had nothing to lose.

In early December, the home owners' secretary called unexpectedly and said that their plans had changed and the place was now available when I wanted it. I'd "caught" my wish! Just keeping my thoughts unwaveringly focused had caused things to shift. How? I don't know. That's the beauty of active meditation: You don't have to understand how it works—that's left to the mystery of the Source.

Actively meditate on the beauty of all God's creations. You are a gorgeous reflection and expression of this Divine Loveliness; all life is dazzling. Reflect on the splendor of your existence today. See how many glorious experiences you can hook and bring into your sphere. Focus on the attractiveness of every individual you see. There is an Eternal Spirit within all beings, and when you actively meditate on the Heavenly Light within others, you draw their grace into your life. People brighten, smile, look you in the eye, and recognize your soul as well. They cooperate, open their hearts to you, and send their creative energy your way. It transforms your world immediately into a friendlier, more positive, and loving place.

Two days ago, I got on a plane to Hawaii on my way to give a talk to a group of people. I was given a seat in the middle section, which wasn't great, but what was far worse was the woman next to me. Horrified by her poor seat assignment, she threw a loud, angry fit. When her antics failed to get her moved, she ranted at the attendant and anyone else who would look at her.

Dismayed at the prospect of sitting next to her hostile energy for the next ten hours, I began to meditate on her beauty. It was difficult to perceive, given her state at the time, so I admired the allure of her rage and passion. With my eyes closed, I maintained my focus during the entire boarding procedure and takeoff. Soon she calmed down and fell asleep. Happily, she didn't wake up for the duration of the trip. When we landed, she looked straight at me and said, "Great flight!" Yes, it had been—for both of us.

Actively meditating on beauty attracts it in every form, and nothing feeds your spirit better. It strengthens and nurtures you on a cellular level. Engage in this contemplation throughout each day. You will become hooked on it.

Now you can apply this lesson.

— If you have no interest in meditation, are too restless and agitated to quietly focus, intend to do so but never get around to it, or think it is a pretentious waste of time . . . then you are a **student** with regard to this lesson.

— If you do not know how to meditate, force yourself to do so sometimes, are curious about the process and want to learn, or sit down to reflect occasionally at best . . . then you are an **apprentice.**

— If you are learning to meditate and like the experience, believe that it is important, rarely worry since you have started this practice, or begin your day with contemplation . . . then you are a **journeyman.**

— If you meditate regularly, notice the beauty in life, are naturally patient, or realize that your focused concentration hooks things from the Divine Sea of Possibility and you love to go fishing . . . then you are on your way to **mastering** this lesson.

If You Are a **Student** . . .

- Pay attention to what you worry about from one day to the next.

- Get a small pocket notebook and write down what you want to focus on.

- Make a collage of your intentions and display it prominently in your home.

- Practice walking meditation: Go for a stroll and notice how many beautiful things are in your life now.

If You Are an **Apprentice** . . .

• Set your alarm clock 15 minutes earlier every morning and use the time to contemplate your intentions for the day.

• Create a simple song or mantra that expresses your desires and sing it as a form of active meditation.

• Get a watch that you can set to beep once per hour. When it goes off, notice what your thoughts are focused on at that moment. Interrupt them if they are counter-productive to your wishes, and change them to align with what you truly want.

• Make a list of all the positive and satisfying things currently going on in your life, and notice how much time you have put into concentrating on these uplifting experiences.

If You Are a **Journeyman** . . .

• In your mind's eye, imagine that you are going fishing and decide to catch something wonderful.

• Before retiring for the evening, spend 10 to15 minutes reviewing all the ways in which God has demonstrated love for you that day. See if the list grows over the period of one week.

• Just before meditating every morning, write down one or two questions and cast them like hooks out into the Universe.

• Be open to "snagging" answers.

- Start to notice all the ideas that flow into your brain during the day, and begin to see how they are delayed responses to your meditative fishing expeditions.

If You Are on Your Way to **Mastering** this Lesson . . .

- Enjoy every day as a positive, creative meditation.

- Set aside ten minutes at noon each day to focus on actively feeling God in your life.

- Every time you need an answer or direction, go fishing during your reflective period, using your question as the hook.

- Look at everything in your life as malleable and fluid, and use your contemplations to reshape the world to be more aligned with what is important and worth creating.

Your Soul's Lesson
Meditation Is Active Creation

Your Soul's Purpose
To Be a Living Meditation of Beauty in This World

Love Your Body

Love your body. Recognize it for what it is: Divine Spirit in physical form. It is a holy creation on the Earth plane, and it should be adored and respected as a beautiful expression of God.

Everything in the material universe is the Creator's handiwork, including your body. Not only is it sacred, it is, in fact, a Heavenly energetic garment that your Inner Being wears. Every corporeal form is a concentrated aspect of Spirit that serves to cloak you in God's beauty.

The idea of loving your flesh-and-blood self may be alien to your way of thinking, especially if you have had early religious training that projected shame upon it. This is a grave error, and damaging to the soul.

When I was a young girl in St. Joseph's Catholic grade school, the other kids and I received regular lectures on how we should cover up our bodies, renounce and repress our physical urges, and never give in to our sexual longings outside of marriage, keeping our thoughts holy and pure instead.

Looking back at these lessons, I understand the instructors' reasoning and motivation, and don't entirely disagree with their intentions, which I feel fairly generous in believing were to protect us from making choices that would harm our spirits. Decisions such as having sex too young or without genuine love and an intimate connection with another can be quite demoralizing, not to mention wreak havoc on the body.

Our moral guides, however, in their zealous manner, stressed to us over and over again that our physical selves were impure, unholy dens of sin. Not surprisingly, this left us feeling anxious and determined to distance ourselves as far as we could from this "ungodly" aspect of ourselves.

After doing psychic readings for more than 30 years, I've come to recognize just how many people suffer deep shame and embarrassment about their bodies. I've witnessed how others struggle, asking me with great hope if they'll ever be able to get "over," "out of," or "away from" their temporary human forms once and for all, thinking that such a renunciation is an indication that they're evolving spiritually.

There is nothing impure or depraved about your living, breathing self. Its functions are remarkable: They are fascinating, sophisticated reflections of the Divine in action, mostly occurring without your conscious mind's awareness.

My husband, Patrick, had this realization when he went back to school at the age of 45 to become a certified massage therapist. After a year of studying anatomy—muscle and nerve construction, blood flow, chemistry, and movement—he developed a reverence and awe for how complex and sophisticated this intricate collection of cells is.

"You can't help but marvel at it," he said, "if for nothing else but the engineering that keeps it going without any conscious thought from us."

Whereas he used to criticize his body out of shortsighted frustration, his training raised his awareness and sensitivity to a whole new level of appreciation and consideration. Now he refuses to speak of his or anyone's human form with anything other than deep regard. In contrast, puritanical notions of judgment and rejection have been around for ages, especially in patriarchal cultures.

Respect and honor how sacred your temporal shell is, for it is truly a temple for the Divine within. It shelters your spirit and gives you a home.

I find that if people aren't busy trying to distance themselves from their bodies because of misguided moral beliefs, they're rejecting and hating themselves because of even more unsound and damaging ideals of what they consider beautiful.

The craziest thing about this singular insanity is that it doesn't even matter what kind of physique you have. In my experience, those who are considered extremely attractive are just as critical and preoccupied with despising their appearances as those who don't have what might be seen as the ideal.

After more than 30 years of experience as an intuitive guide, I'd say that this lack of acceptance is perhaps the number one psychic problem people struggle with. To my horror, I see this epidemic afflicting increasingly younger individuals—especially girls.

I just did a reading for a gorgeous 11-year-old whose mother brought her to see me because she's obsessed with feeling fat, even though her weight is in the normal range. Because of her delusion, she started refusing to eat. Her perceptions of beauty, especially of her own, were hijacked in her first year of middle school, where the standards were dictated by teen magazines, MTV, and the most popular students in the upper grades. Her body, unfortunately, didn't conform to these ideals, so she decided that it was unacceptable and started hating it.

That's absurd, you might say, especially for someone her age, but most adults I've met are just as preoccupied with rejecting themselves for the same reasons. The highest-ranked obsession for most women over 25 is dieting, and the numbers of people seeking plastic surgery for cosmetic reasons alone are now reaching the hundreds of thousands.

I explained to my young client that her human form was a sacred garment for her spirit, and that it was to be loved and cherished rather than treated with contempt and disgust.

But when I asked her what she thought of her body, she said, without a moment's hesitation, "I hate it." She had no appreciation or understanding that it's a heavenly vessel for the soul, and couldn't accept what I said. In her mind, it was a stubborn, ugly mass of flesh and bones that she was trapped in and couldn't control.

It took quite a lengthy conversation before she was willing to see it another way. After a great deal of reflecting, she was finally able to consider her physical self as part of her Inner Essence rather than something smothering it, but the realization didn't come easily.

Be grounded and content in your own skin. Your body is your personal temple, and it provides peace, power, and protection. This has nothing to do with its shape, size, or features. It is a Divine container for Spirit to rest within. Each of you is a unique manifestation of God, and your earthly form is perfect for you.

To get a better idea of how ideas and emotions shape physical expression, think about renting the movie What the Bleep Do We Know!?, *an exciting documentary on thought, feeling, and physical reality. It explains that if you see your body as an ugly, contemptible, unruly lump of flesh, you'll create a physical reality that eventually reflects that very belief.*

The temple of the spirit, like everything else in the material world, is not solid. It is fluid and malleable and conforms to whatever mental vision and feelings you hold about it. If you despise your body, it will reflect your hatred through aches, pains, and illness. If you love it and treat it tenderly, it will mirror your attitude by having vitality, strength, and health.

My client Elray was born with one leg two inches shorter than the other. He has worn a special shoe to compensate for the imbalance ever since he could walk. He was fortunate because, since infancy, his grandmother constantly told him that his guardian angels had pulled his leg when he was born, trying to bring him to Earth, while he wanted to play in heaven, causing one limb to be longer than the other. She hugged and kissed him, and thanked him for finally agreeing to let the celestial messengers succeed in bringing him to her. This story delighted and enchanted him, and made him feel lucky.

Not surprisingly, when he began school, the other children taunted him about his appearance, but he didn't care. He told them with great pride about the angels and that he was quite happy about his shorter leg. His confidence fascinated them and made him a hero. Not only did Elray refuse to buy into others' ideas of attractiveness, he fully accepted his unique beauty without apology. He thought his leg was wonderful and he walked with confidence.

The kids stopped their rejection of him as it fell on deaf ears, and they fell in love with him instead. He was a star in their eyes. Elray defied all the rules about what's appealing and dared to adore himself as he was, the way his grandmother did. Such an enlightened decision made his life a joy and set him apart as an example of what it means to be truly embodied in Spirit.

After his first son turned three, Elray called me. "Would you believe that my little boy came home crying from preschool today? He told his friends about my legs and the angel story and all. He wanted to know why one of his legs wasn't shorter than the other, like mine. He wanted a sign that his heavenly guardians had tugged on him as well."

"What did you say?" I asked.

"I pointed to his big ears and said that they pulled on those instead. He was delighted."

Appreciate and even marvel at the work of art that is your physical vehicle. Without conscious effort on your part, your brain fires, your heart pumps, your organs cleanse and nourish you, your stomach digests, your skin breathes, and a million other amazing functions flow naturally.

Your body allows you to speak, think, sing, move, feel, express, and take full pleasure in the Earth plane. It is a miraculous and perfect instrument for your soul's evolution; and is to be completely loved, respected, and enjoyed.

Be grateful for all the wonderful things your physical self affords you. It is an incredible tool for growing your spirit, and it mirrors your choices so that you can see, feel, and experience exactly what you are manifesting at all times.

It is the ideal means for expressing your imaginative power. Being out of body after death does not allow you to bypass these evolutionary lessons, as some people wrongly believe. All it does is give you a temporary rest until you regain energy and are ready to reenter the material arena, take on another human form, and continue learning how to become a creative master.

You cannot aspire to higher levels of consciousness until you are peaceful in your present physical awareness. Your body is your best teacher because it precisely reflects how you are viewing yourself. This does not mean that you are to strive to become an ideal specimen of beauty or health—especially according to other people's standards. Instead, realize that you are already perfect in God's eyes, and love your Divine temple completely.

My client Fred didn't care for his body for many years. In fact, he made harmful choices for most of his adult life. He smoked, drank excessively, overworked, rarely gave himself down time, and ate food with little to no nutritional value. This went on until he was 59. Then one day at work, he had a stroke. Luckily, one of his co-workers recognized what was happening and got him to a hospital in less than 15 minutes. He received treatment quickly enough that he suffered no long-term disabilities.

He was so shocked at his vulnerability and grateful to everyone who worked to save him that he had an epiphany: Because he'd been spared, he vowed to change his ways and treat his body better.

Fred quit smoking, drinking, and eating carelessly. He began exercising and stopped working weekends. He suddenly loved life and the fact that he was still breathing, and wanted to keep going in a vehicle that functioned well. He didn't give up his self-destructive behaviors out of fear or submission to his doctor's warnings. He did it because he decided to be good to himself out of appreciation for not dying or becoming handicapped from the stroke.

He said that it wasn't even hard. "While I was 'out of it,' I had a talk with God," he explained. "He asked me if I wanted to live. I said yes, of course, and I heard in response, 'Then show it by being good to your body.' That's all it took. I'm a changed man—and a healthier, happier one."

Never say an unkind word about your physical form. Do not call it fat, slow, ugly, old, wrinkled, too tall, too short, too bald, or too thin. Love it as is and appreciate how tenderly it serves you. Know your body, for each one has its own requirements for balance and health. What are yours? Care for it and listen to what it needs for balance. Also notice what you put in this amazing instrument of life. Is it good for you? Or does it harm you? To know the answers is a reflection of love.

My neighbor Susan remarked one day that she didn't feel great after she ate meat. It was a simple awareness that she finally acknowledged. By giving up this food, she felt 100 percent better.

I, on the other hand, quit eating meat for several years and became sick, tired, and weak. I paid attention and discovered that adding it back to my diet was important.

My husband, Patrick, and daughter Sabrina both need a lot of tradi-tional aerobic activity to feel good. My daughter Sonia does better with yoga and sleep in the morning.

There's no one-size-fits-all way to care for your body, apart from supplying the basics, of course—good sleep, plenty of water, nutritious food, and exercise. Listen to it, and it will tell you what it needs.

In addition to your corporeal self, you also have mental and emotional bodies that need care. Positive thoughts, gratitude, self-respect, and self-appreciation are fuel for the mental entity, while compliments, laughter, time to relax, and social fun are sustenance for the emotional one.

My extroverted husband needs social gatherings, while I, the intro-vert, need to spend time alone. We're all unique in what we need to nurture our bodies.

Tell yourself, "I love you" every time you see your reflection. Never say that you hate yourself, or use the word *hate* in referring to your body, for it is a Divine cloak of light. It can be reshaped into any form you wish. It is responsive, resilient, hardy, forgiving, and absolutely honest. It will adapt to the image you hold—not immediately, but soon enough. To naturally mold your physical self into a vessel that pleases you—without the use of plastic sur-gery, liposuction, or other extreme makeovers—give it adoration and appreciation, steadily maintain the vision you seek in your mind and heart, and choose behaviors that support your desired outcome. Cherish your sacred vehicle, and it will love you back.

One final note: We wish to address deformities, chronic illness, birth defects, and diseases, and how to love your body when faced with these challenges. As we have said before, the Earth plane is the greatest arena for spiritual evolution and expansion of the soul. When a person is faced with a physical difficulty, it represents an opportunity for the spirit to grow in a particular way. It may be a chance to learn to let go of control or to develop on other levels. On the other hand, sometimes the purpose of a certain disability or illness is not to serve the personal growth of the afflicted individual, but to strengthen the Divine qualities in those around the person. In this case, it is a soul choice made to help others. Or the reason for the experience may be for the individual in question to learn to accept love from others.

Whatever the particular lesson of any handicap, disorder, or chronic or catastrophic disease may be, it is a teaching tool chosen by the Higher Self to support its purpose. Respect this decision and learn from it without judgment.

I had a client whose series of physical and emotional disabilities seemed never ending. But in spite of his challenges, or maybe because of them, he learned two critical soul lessons: first, to surrender his personal ego to God instead of being controlling; and second, to receive and accept the love of others, especially those who treated and nurtured him. Many other people were also given gifts because of his illnesses. It wasn't a simple situation. When it comes to health issues, it never is.

In caring for all three bodies—mental, emotional, and physical—love is the best medicine. Treat your body tenderly, care for it sensibly, and speak to it with respect. Wear it proudly as your personal Divine cloak of Spirit.

Now you can apply the lesson.

— If you criticize your body, often say "I hate" when referring to it, harm it with toxic substances, or disregard its basic needs and push it too hard . . . then you are a **student** in learning this lesson.

— If you try to accept your physical form; occasionally pay attention to what you put in it; think about exercising and getting adequate rest even if you do not actually do so; or recognize that what you eat, drink, and do affects your constitution . . . then you are an **apprentice.**

— If you are conscientious about the care of your body, think of it kindly and accept the appreciation and compliments of others graciously, seek to create a positive atmosphere wherever you are, or refrain from comparing your human form to others and are simply grateful to be in your unique vehicle . . . then you are a **journeyman.**

— If you bless your body often; listen to its messages; pamper it; love being in your own skin; and make healthy, caring choices for your flesh-and-blood self every day . . . then you are on your way to **mastering** this lesson.

If You Are a **Student** . . .

- Pay attention to your body and how it reacts to what you eat, drink, do, and think.

- Keep notes of your observations.

- Tell your earthly self "I love you" often.

- Place love notes on every mirror and reflective surface in your home.

- Never say unkind words about your physical form, especially "I hate . . . " If you slip up, say out loud "Cancel, cancel."

- Take at least one day off each week to rest, meditate, go for a walk, and relax.

If You Are an **Apprentice** . . .

- Exercise 15 minutes a day.

- Eat wholesome food.

- Drink more water.

- Give up one negative habit, such as smoking, drinking excessively, or eating too much meat or sugar.

- Regularly compliment yourself out loud.

If You Are a **Journeyman** . . .

- Start every morning with a few deep breaths and gentle stretches, and tell your body how grateful you are for its service to you.

- Give your physical self regular treats as a loving gesture, such as a massage; a warm, luxurious bath; or a relaxing cup of your favorite tea. Acknowledge out loud that you are pampering yourself.

- Speak kindly about your Divine form to yourself and others whenever the subject arises.

- Notice how your surroundings affect your body, and remove yourself from negative or stressful environments as quickly as possible out of consideration for yourself.

If You Are on Your Way to **Mastering** this Lesson . . .

- Notice the activities your body loves and do at least one every day, such as dancing, napping, stretching, walking, holding hands with a loved one, listening to good music, or eating a leisurely meal.

- Pay keen attention to your diet and only consume what leaves you feeling good.

- Eat and drink in smaller portions so as not to overtax the intricate functioning of your organs.

- Pray, meditate, and contemplate the magnificence of your body and how it serves you every day, and thank it out loud often.

Your Soul's Lesson
Your Body Is Holy

Your Soul's Purpose
To Proudly Live in Your Earthly Cloak of Spirit

Regenerate Your Soul

R egenerate your soul, your inner light, by connecting to the Living Sun, which is your source and the giver of life on your planet. It is not merely an impersonal fiery orb of gas, but a form of Vital Consciousness that affords you and all organisms on Earth the ability to sustain yourselves. Without it, you simply could not exist.

Within the burning, physical sun is a consciousness—an intense, loving vibration that radiates to your world to activate, awaken, and maintain your spirit. You have a corresponding center in your body to receive and amass this life force of light: your heart. It is the equivalent of the sun in your flesh-and-blood self. It collects energy from the Shimmering Source, then sends it into every one of your cells. The more brilliance that you gather and transmit to all the parts of your being, the healthier, happier, and more enlightened you become.

When your soul absorbs light, you can actually sense and even see it in and around the body. You have a sparkle in your eyes, your aura is bright, your smile flashes, and you are said to shine. You also channel a higher level of life force into the energy field surrounding your physical self. You become attractive and magnetic. This greater influx of power illuminates your aura and draws others to you in the same way that plugging in festive lights on a Christmas tree captivates people.

Respect the Sun as a Being of Transcendent Essence that supports you. Just as the earth is a living consciousness that we call *Gaia*—the Divine Mother—your star is also a Sacred Consciousness known as your Heavenly Father. You are children dancing in the Holy Light. Gather it in to sustain yourselves.

Ancient, advanced civilizations, such as those developed by the Egyptians and the Aztecs, recognized your connection to the Living Sun. They worshipped it and built structures and wore jewelry to help collect its radiance in their bodies. You may dismiss these cultures as superstitious and silly, but they were not. Their creations and accomplishments were so sophisticated that to this day they stump scholars and architects who cannot figure out how they achieved what they did.

About 15 years ago, Patrick and I took a second trip to Egypt, where we'd gotten engaged 10 years earlier. This time, we toured on a cruise down the Nile. At one point, we stopped in the Valley of the Kings and were led out of the endless sand dunes into a vast and quite spectacular tomb that extended for miles.

It was extremely difficult to understand not only how it was built, but how its creators had been able to see well enough to paint the elaborate hieroglyphics that covered the walls. They were brightly colored and appeared as though they'd been finished the day before, even though the vaults were constructed thousands of years ago.

The guide explained that an intricate system of highly polished bronze plates was used to reflect the sun's illumination deep into the tunnels. At the time, I thought it was clever, but found it difficult to fully conceive. Now I understand that to create such profound beauty, the Egyptians refracted the Eternal rays of love deep into the ground, almost like a holy sexual union between Gaia, the Divine feminine, and the Sun, the Glorious masculine. It was more than engineering. These people knew what they were doing on every level, and to this day, the burial chambers stand as a testimonial to the power of channeling light.

The Living Sun gives you the ability to achieve your full potential. Its vibration is the very specific motion of unlimited, unconditional love. It sustains you. It pours into the earth, fills the plants, and becomes your fuel. It creates your food sources as well as your building materials. It also streams into your body, causing it to produce the vitamin D that builds your bones, skin, eyes, teeth, and muscle density.

It is not enough to amass sun energy in your physical self or ingest it via your nutritional sources, although this does keep you going at the most basic level. You must bring this same light into your consciousness—your mental and emotional bodies—to truly evolve into an enlightened being. You do this through your heart.

This center of the human form corresponds to the sun in the solar system. Your emotional core is your personal sun and is the collector of Divine Light from the Living Star. When your heart is open, it naturally gathers the life force into your system every time you go outdoors. It then amplifies and mirrors this energy outward, directing this light (love) beyond the self to others. This process regenerates you on every level: mind, body, and spirit.

Once your physical self is filled with luminescence, you become a tremendous generator of love for others by sending it into the world. The more your heart is regenerated, the more you can accumulate a deep well of adoration and caring inside yourself. As a result, you become a better giver and evolve into a greater Light Being, thus fulfilling your purpose.

In addition, the more radiant energy you gather, the more sensitive you become to the vibrations around you. This heightened—or more accurately, *enlightened*—awareness causes you to become more selective in your choices.

You will first notice a desire for more light in your diet, and you will naturally be drawn to foods that contain high amounts of sun energy, such as fruits, vegetables, and grains. This is why so often you choose to become a vegetarian once you begin to raise your awareness of your purpose. The more you eat these kinds of things, the more light and love you deliver to your cells. This does not mean that you must stop eating meat; however, it does not contain light—only those items grown from the sun do.

You may also observe a change in the kind of clothing you prefer. The more aware you become of gathering solar energy into your physical self, the more attracted you will be to wearing light-colored fabrics, because they reflect more brilliance from the body. This is why so many spiritually aware people prefer white or bright shades to dark tones. Even nuns and priests who don black habits and frocks surround their faces or throats with white collars or wimples to amplify the light of their expression.

This does not mean that somber garments are unacceptable; we simply seek to make you conscious that they block the radiance, so wear them with prudence.

You become sensitive to your environment as well. You need adequate illumination in your atmosphere in order to thrive. Dark places with poor or artificial light are draining to your soul and physical body, as are long, dreary, gray winter spells.

Fortunately, collective awareness about our need for proper light to rejuvenate ourselves has given rise to a specialized field. Now you can purchase full-spectrum lightbulbs, which produce the kind of rays we need to regenerate ourselves. Just get on the Internet and Google "full-spectrum lightbulbs," and you'll have access to every kind available.

You will also become more sensitive to energetic ambience. Dark energy is detrimental to your cells and slows your soul's growth. Your spirit cannot tolerate dissonant, unloving, or tense vibrations for long without experiencing a drain on its energy. When faced with a negative, dreary atmosphere, try to brighten things up by being "lighthearted." If this does not change the mood, quickly remove yourself.

When my client Annie was a new doctor, she discovered that everyone in her clinic was extremely closed hearted and often consumed with a dark mood. They were critical of one another, the patients, and other physicians, and had nothing nice or pleasant to say about anything. They showed up late, were defensive when confronted, and resentful when asked to do their jobs properly.

Annie's efforts to lighten things up might well have been met with steel trapdoors: She was shut out, her radiant spirit was rejected, and she was dragged down by the lack of light and love.

After five months, she was seriously suffering from their psychic dreariness. It made her irritable, depressed, and even angry. As hard as it was, she chose to leave, thus postponing fulfilling her residency requirements for another year.

"My brain said stay, but I couldn't because the energy was so gloomy there," she explained.

Annie did the right thing. She had to go because she needed a lighter, more loving vibration. This decision caused her to switch from family medicine to pediatrics, and although it was a longer road, it filled her heart.

Although sunlight is essential to your physical and soul bodies, too much can be overtaxing, and unbridled energy presents problems. Despite the fact that collecting illumination (love) is a fundamental requirement for the spirit to achieve its highest vibration as a Light Being, there is a risk of garnering too much brilliance, intensity, and passion at one time, throwing your system into overload.

Even though you need the sun to sustain life, in places where Earth's natural filters have been burned away, nonstop radiation becomes too strong, threatening to destroy the planet with its fiery force. This is why you now require sunblock and other protectors to guard against overexposure to the concentration of solar energy.

This year alone, I've met with more than 20 clients under the age of 40 who have skin cancer. Most of them, in one way or another, were sun worshippers in the past, not thinking twice about spending hours and hours baking outdoors in order to get a good tan, often without using any protection at all. Needless to say, not only was their skin damaged and eventually sickened, this extreme exposure now threatened other parts of their body with cancer as well. It was shocking to them, and to me.

Part of the problem is our general lack of respect for the power of the sun and our inattention to how it affects us on a physical level. In addition, our public policies have allowed us to destroy the ozone layer, which up until now has guarded us from the intensity of our Living Sun God. Sooner or later, we'll realize our mistakes and hopefully be able to correct them before we're all endangered by cancer.

You need light every day to regenerate, but it is not necessary or wise to bask outside for hours on end. About 20 minutes is more than adequate. In the same way, it is important to moderate your expenditure of sun energy, which translates into fire, fuel, and enthusiasm. When you express too much zeal and do not temper its force, you are said to be burning the candle at both ends. When you fail to restrain yourself in spite of all warnings, your nervous system becomes overtaxed and shuts down—a syndrome you call "burnout." In these situations, you collect and dissipate solar power nonstop but fail to offset your soul with moon energy or quiet receptivity, thus creating imbalance.

I just read in USA Today *that more than 70 percent of the population is suffering from sleep deprivation and overwork. In fact, exhaustion and too little slumber was cited as the number one problem for most professional workers worldwide. Obviously, a great many of us need to learn to shut off the lights and relax, including me. If we don't do this, the sun energy we've collected can't be assimilated to regenerate our minds, bodies, and spirits.*

Although it is important and essential for your physical, mental, emotional, and soul bodies to be regenerated by the sun on a daily basis, once you have replenished yourself, you must retreat and assimilate it quietly. The same goes for expressing sun energy in the form of enthusiasm and effort. Be passionate but keep it contained and do not let it overwhelm you.

Follow the example of the Living Sun for guidance. It rises every day on schedule, infusing you with measured light energy. Then it recedes so that you can process and digest what you are fed. You do not need to be nourished nonstop. Instead, you must rest and have quiet, contemplative respites. Be aware of the mind's inclination to overexpress, overdo, and overintend, thus burning up all your solar fuel and causing you to collapse or become fatigued, exhausted, or drained—your most common Earth ailments at this time.

As a conscious Divine Being, be mindful of how much light you collect in a 24-hour period. Remember that the only way to gather it into the body is to bring an open heart to the Sun every day. Is yours receptive? If not, you are starving your soul of its basic food and most likely feeling the effects. Set your intention to collect 20 minutes a day to regenerate your cells and spirit. You will notice the difference immediately.

One of the greatest purposes of your Higher Self is to be a beacon to others. How much do you radiate? Do you bring energy to others, or are you a grim shadow? Do you shine out, or are you full of doom and gloom? Giving and sharing illumination and love is your reason for being. Casting darkness blocks life and drains your and others' vital force, setting you back. An enlightened being is literally one who sends forth light and affection to the planet, and your soul's destiny is to evolve and become such an ambassador.

You are here to learn to be an Enlightened or Light Being. The Lord of the Universe decreed, "Let there be light." This is the most succinct directive of your purpose on Earth that you will find. It is all very simple if you recognize that light is love.

Now you can apply this lesson.

— If you are full of doom and gloom, sit in the dark, constantly wear somber colors, push yourself too hard, or eat mindlessly and avoid the sun . . . then you are a **student** with regard to this lesson.

— If you recognize the need to take things less seriously but find it difficult; are sensitive to the ambience of a place and react negatively when the lights are poor or not bright enough; are burned out and feel lifeless; are attracted to cheerful, easygoing people even if your energy is dark; or prefer vegetables and fruits to steaks . . . then you are an **apprentice.**

— If you feel a sudden attraction to lighter colors and brighter light; are inclined to be vegetarian; like to sunbathe, keep the blinds open, and fill your rooms with sunshine; or know when to stop, rest, and regenerate, then you are a **journeyman.**

— If you radiate your spirit out into the world, remain upbeat and optimistic no matter what occurs, go outside daily to take in the sun, or cheer people up and brighten their days . . . then you are well on your way to **mastering** this lesson.

If You Are a **Student** . . .

- Purchase full-spectrum lightbulbs and install them around your home and workplace.

- Take a daily 20-minute walk outside, and wear sunblock.

- Open the blinds and shades and let the sun in.

- Wear light-colored clothing to reflect more illumination from your body.

If You Are an **Apprentice** . . .

- Eat more vegetables, fruits, and whole grains.

- Open your heart and forgive those against whom you hold grudges.

- Reposition your furniture to sit and sleep near windows.

- Repaint your walls to reflect more light, and add mirrors and crystals to refract even more.

If You Are a **Journeyman** . . .

- Intentionally infuse others with the radiance of your open spirit.

- Sit outdoors and work in the sun for 15 to 20 minutes a day.

- Wear gold or crystals near your heart to gather more solar energy into your body.

- Remove yourself immediately from all toxic environments.

If You Are on Your Way to **Mastering** this Lesson . . .

- Bring light to situations and people.

- Check local spas for infrared saunas and treat yourself to a visit.

- Wear white on the upper part of your body at least three times a week.

- Keep your heart open by taking nothing and no one personally.

Your Soul's Lesson
Let the Sunshine In

Your Soul's Purpose
To Bring More Light into the World

Shatter Negative Patterns

Everything in your world is created by repeating patterns. Starting with the zygote at conception, cells divide millions of times. This process is responsible for the development of all physical bodies. In fact, all of life is based on various kinds of duplication. If you study a plant closely, you see that the leaves contain arrangements of energy that recur over and over again. This is also true in the realm of construction. Buildings and houses are all composed of rhythmic designs of brick, mortar, steel, and so on. Your physical experience is generated by the repetition.

Patterns are powerful when the results that are replicated are sound, good, and positive. It only becomes a problem when the process does not lead to a desirable outcome. Like a computer program running with an error, you will continue to create the same negative effects until you fix the glitch. To correct your energetic mistakes, you must dismantle the old paradigm and replace it with an improved one.

This is done in three stages. Stage One is to become aware of or identify the offending pattern. Whether it involves an unhealthy body, lack in the material world, or unsatisfactory relationships, simply recognize it on an impersonal level as something that has gone awry. Be objective and perceive the unhappy condition with neutrality. Nothing is working against you. Your program just has a flaw that needs to be repaired.

Stage Two is to understand the origin of your habitual behavior or way of thinking. Patterns are adopted, whether from your early childhood environment, previous lives, or present social conditioning. Try to locate the source, because this helps you see how this situation has served you in the past and why you embraced it in the first place.

In the case of my overwork tendency, I recognize it as one I learned from my father. Because he modeled this pattern every day when I was a child, it's easy to understand how I adopted it so easily as a way of life. Studying it, I see that to some degree, at least until recently, it has been helpful and has served me well. After all, it pushed me to write many books in a short period of time; teach and travel all over the world while raising two daughters; operate a consulting practice; and maintain a marriage to a temperamental, artistic, and sometimes demanding man—all at the same time. That was a lot of work.

But now that my daughters are grown, my relationship with my husband is less challenging, and my schedule is relaxing, this tradition no longer serves me, which is why it has to go. Now that my desires have shifted, I have to take action to create change.

Once you are aware of an undesirable pattern, recognize that it first exists as a mental vibration or blueprint held in your subconscious mind. To change unwanted habits, you must alter this internal energy framework and establish the updated one in its place. This is accomplished through consistency. It is not enough to think positively from time to time. Instead, you must *permanently* replace old cognitive habits with new ones, resisting any temptation to return to the outmoded way.

When dismantling obsolete patterns and trading them in for more desirable ones, recognize that they have simply outgrown their usefulness. The key is not to judge any of your behavioral or thinking modes as bad—just accept that they are no longer appropriate given your current wishes. If you condemn them, you become emotionally hooked, which makes them stick like glue. Judgment attaches, while nonjudgment detaches, so do not be critical—just observe.

Stage Three is to let go of the emotional responses that went along with the original mental blueprint and embody new ones that correspond with your higher intention. Stop reacting automatically, and instead choose an approach that reflects your new desire or purpose.

For me, this meant confronting the belief I'd carried all my life that overwork was righteous and good—something I was rewarded for and that made me feel like a superior person. I had to reset my mental vibrations to correspond with my new decision, which meant I had to stop becoming overwhelmed with guilt the minute I ceased working and instead develop a positive view of rest. It also meant surrendering the pride I carried about my near-Olympic ability to toil away on a project without taking a break for days—or even weeks, if necessary—and recognize it as self-destructive vanity.

None of this came easy. After all, I'd invested many years, and even lifetimes, in these patterns, which were very familiar and served as a source of self-satisfaction, something my unconscious ego was not too eager to give up. In fact, one of the reasons I think I chose the family I did in this incarnation was because it offered me a chance to reengage this habitual workaholism, having carried it over from a past life or two. Because all of my relatives drove themselves so hard, it felt very much like home. I had to train myself to feel good about relaxing. It was a new experience, but I liked it.

You transfer programs from one lifetime to the next, letting go of bodies and circumstances, but not behaviors—at least not automatically. You can only consciously change yourself by shattering the old pattern according to the three aforementioned stages. Your most fundamental soul lesson on Earth is to quickly transform what no longer serves you. This is the only place in the Universe where you can break self-defeating, restrictive habits and learn, through trial and error, to become the Creative Immortal Light Being that you are.

The quickest way to demolish a response sequence is to "fake it until you make it," because the subconscious mind cannot distinguish the real from the perceived. A case in point is lemons. Think of biting into one and see what happens. You immediately pucker up and cringe from the very thought. That is because, to your unconscious, you really are sinking your teeth into a sour fruit. The same thing occurs when you focus on being joyful. Even if you do not feel happy at the moment, if you start acting as if you are, your mind gets fooled and automatically starts creating bliss. Try this right now and you will see how it works.

Emotions are habits, just like behaviors. Implementing new ones is simply a matter of changing your routines. Practice feeling positive and optimistic about your new manifestations, even if you think you are simply going through the motions or "faking it." Remember that emotions are the fuel for creativity. Knowing this, you can choose powerful ones that lead to amazing results.

I had a client who never felt attractive or noticed by others. Accepting this as a pattern rather than a fixed reality, she decided to create "being beautiful" instead. With her new blueprint in mind, she practiced feeling gorgeous. One way she did this was to avoid mirrors and ignore her present physical appearance. Other than a few minutes in the morning as she got ready for work, she avoided looking at her reflection throughout the day. She did, however, focus on lovely emotions around the clock. The more she did so, the more she radiated her new vibration. It took only three weeks to start receiving compliments from others—even strangers—on how alluring she was.

The next step is to change your behavior. If you want to shatter a pattern you must *do* something different. Furthermore, you cannot just make an effort once or twice and expect results; you must permanently replace the old way of acting with a new one.

I came across the following compelling statement in the ancient Nordic oracle the <u>Book of Runes.</u> "There is only one power in the Universe and that is the power of decision. All else follows."

Once you decide to shatter a pattern, the Universe immediately steps in to support you in the form of synchronicities, inspiration, opportunity, and renewed vitality. God cannot impose your Divinity upon you; you must choose it. The minute you do so, you open the way for heavenly power to serve you.

You are the master of your life, but you do have guides, angels, and our Loving Creator available to aid you. Change paradigms with the knowledge that the Sacred is working with you. There is a saying that goes something like: "When God is with you nothing is against you."

Humor helps you transform behaviors faster than any other energy. Laugh at them—with affection, of course, but do have a chuckle. None of them really holds any power over you. You give them influence through your attention, but you can also take it back. You might struggle to do this, but you do not have to. You can detach from the pattern far more easily by making light of your habits. Other ways are effective, but using wit works much more quickly.

My client Forrest had the self-destructive pattern of dating shallow and manipulative women who used him for his money, then dumped him. After a series of humiliating heartbreaks, he decided to join an improvisational comedy group and make fun of his love life instead of continuing to suffer the same mistakes over and over again. He figured that it would be cheaper and less harmful to his already crushed ego and that he had nothing to lose.

In a matter of just a few weeks, Forrest had turned his emotional misery into a hilarious routine that captivated and tickled the funny bones of the audiences every night. Poking fun at his woes turned him into an instant success. Suddenly he found himself swamped with offers from ladies who saw his show and wanted to go out with him.

A few months after he launched his act, he started seeing someone he'd met in the same improv ensemble who'd had an equally painful love life before turning to comedy. They formed a duet that focused on dating tribulations and brought the house down with laughter. The last I heard, they'd gotten married and had stopped performing.

Have patience, for shattering patterns and implementing new ones takes time. It is like changing what grows in your garden: You must first uproot the old plants, then put in the seeds and wait on the Universe. It may take several seasons before the old shrubs and flowers are completely cleared and the new ones are fully in bloom, but it will happen.

Before the Light Beings began to pour onto the planet to assist your collective soul purpose, a person would normally experience three life cycles before successfully dismantling one self-defeating behavior. However, the earth cannot support such slow progress anymore. That is why we encourage you to laugh at everything that is no longer desired, because it elevates the spirit and the world more quickly. We are giggling with you!

Having said this, we understand how difficult it is to be mirthful when your soul is in pain. Yet suffering is the greatest catalyst for your evolution. After all, when everything is going well, you are less inclined to connect with your true nature. It is only when you ache, feel sorrow, and experience loss that you become genuinely interested in making changes.

We hope that you will alter your perspective on anguish and see it as a spur to transformation. Reposition it in your mind as a teacher and friend. When you observe or experience affliction, evaluate it accurately. Do not judge it as "bad." Simply accept it as your indication that it is time to grow.

Pain stimulates development. Once you learn your lesson, you no longer need the hurt and can let it go. Do not fall into the habit of being perpetually wounded. We witness again and again how you hang on to torment as though clinging to a security blanket.

Notice how accurately you can describe your last distressing experience and even re-create the feelings. Then, as an exercise in awareness, tell about the most recent positive event in your life. Nine times out of ten, you cannot recount the wonderful things with anywhere near the intensity with which you recall the disagreeable ones.

My client Marie went through the agonizing dissolution of her marriage and a divorce. She was bankrupted by her husband, who left her for another woman, and abandoned by his adult children from a previous relationship. Although it was devastating, she had known when she married him that he was incapable of fidelity or honesty. She'd also realized that his kids were manipulative and self-serving as a result of having a father like him. However, she entered the scene believing that she could change all of them.

Knowing now just how hard transforming one's own patterns and vibrations can be—let alone those of other people—Marie finally recognized how ludicrous her plan had been. The divorce ultimately brought her back to her senses. The suffering she experienced while married enabled her to let go and stop forcing her idea of growth on her family while ignoring her own development.

The problem she now creates for herself is that of constantly retelling the story of her woes to anyone who will listen. It's as though she's addicted to retraumatizing herself on a daily basis.

When I asked her why she keeps inflicting this old misery on herself, Marie said that she wanted to make certain that she never commits the same errors again.

The absurdity of her reasoning is that in her perpetual recounting of past events, she energetically relives the same blunders. When I suggested that she let it go, she lashed out, exclaiming, "Never!"

Her intense resistance unveiled her love of suffering, and I understood her. Her dwelling on the past excused her from getting back in the game of life and continuing her growth. I didn't push her to change, though. Evolution can be as fast or slow as we decide. Apparently, she's in no hurry.

When you are in pain and unable to detach, examine, and consciously shift your patterning, we offer another tool to help you: the use of sound, which is made up of vibrations. By singing or chanting certain mantras, you can generate vibrations that are higher than those of the behavior or thought you wish to transform. Doing this practice long enough will shatter a harmful program and free the energy to create a new one.

Two powerful mantras are *Om mane padme um* (I am that I am) and *A-do-na-I* (pronounced *A-do-na-ee*), which means "God in the physical plane." Chant these sacred formulas in any fashion you choose. Find your own key, tone, and rhythm, and let the sound do the work.

Sing *A-do-na-I* a maximum of three times while focusing on what you want to overcome, such as isolation, poverty, or illness. Your mantra becomes a focused vibration that disturbs the existing energy field. Do this several times throughout the day and you will observe a shift within 3 to 30 days.

Om mane padme um can be chanted as long and as often as you like for the same purpose. Every time you are faced with a behavior that no longer serves you, causes pain, or keeps you from being present, chant *Om mane padme um* while holding the distressing habit in your mind. This practice disrupts the situation by calling on the name of God.

Another way to shatter outworn patterns is to invoke the archangel Gabriel by singing his name, pronouncing it *Ga-bree-el*. One of his specific purposes is to help you break old personal paradigms and release new ones into expression, so feel free to call upon him whenever you desire assistance.

I find that when using mantras and chants or invoking Gabriel, it helps to understand what happens to a pattern when a higher vibration is introduced. In the 1970s, there was a TV commercial advertising Memorex cassette tapes. The ad showed a crystal goblet. Then, jazz singer Ella Fitzgerald began to sing, and the resonance of her voice was so high—higher than the oscillation of the molecules that held the vessel together—that the object shattered.

What wasn't apparent was that before the crystal fragmented, the molecules that made up the goblet contracted, holding on tightly to one another in an attempt to maintain their order. It took the sustained note—or higher frequency—to break through and release the constriction.

This phenomenon occurs throughout nature and in our lives. When an elevated energy is introduced to any established formulation, it first retracts in an effort to preserve itself. This is why the minute people decide to go on a diet or give up cigarettes, their immediate response is to devour everything in sight or smoke like a fiend. The atoms, molecules, and mental and emotional resonance sequences react by fighting for their existence.

This is the best time to introduce a higher vibration. Instead of eating, for example, sing <u>Om mane padme um</u> or call on Gabriel three times; then go for a walk, clean your closet, or do something different. The same technique works for quitting smoking: Rather than inhaling, chant <u>A-do-na-I</u> three times; then breathe, stretch, and take a walk. You can invoke these energies for any behavior you want to change. All of *these mantras elicit a greater resonance to fight the contraction, shatter the pattern, and release a new power.*

As we have stated, as a spiritual being, you are connected to everyone and everything in the Universe. Consequently, you deeply affect others—and vice versa. Your pain is another's, and theirs is yours. Look at any suffering, past or present, as your personal opportunity to transcend for the whole of humanity. You carry the hurt for all, and you transcend it for everyone as well. Going beyond your heartache and becoming a joyful being of light is the highest contribution you can make to your fellow humans. You become a living example of what is possible that others can follow. The more tribulations you overcome, the more love you bring to others. As you know, your greatest purpose is to serve the whole as an enlightened ambassador. And the only way to do so is to work through the hindrance and darkness of outworn patterns and move on to a higher vibration.

Now you can apply the lesson.

— If you are a mindless creature of obsolete habits, make no effort to examine your behavior for counterproductive patterns, constantly re-create the frustrations and pain of the past, or feel stuck . . . then you are a **student** in learning this lesson.

— If you notice that you have some negative programming, seek counsel on those parts of your life that are unfulfilling, resist change, or hope that things will get better . . . then you are an **apprentice.**

— If you are transforming various aspects of yourself, are sticking with new choices even if you are not getting instant results, realize that growth takes time and are willing to be patient, or feel inspired to sing or chant to invoke a higher vibration . . . then you are a **journeyman.**

— If you seek to resonate with elevated levels of energy, confront self-defeating behaviors head-on, or keep a positive attitude in the midst of upheaval . . . then you are well on your way to **mastering** this lesson.

If You Are a **Student** . . .

- Ask yourself if you want to change.

- Be aware of your pain and see it as a call to growth.

- Listen to CD recordings of the chant *Om mane padme um.*

- Ask others what patterns they see repeating in your life.

- Pay attention to what depresses you or causes you to feel hopeless, and notice what you are doing when these dark vibrations sweep over you.

If You Are an **Apprentice** . . .

- Identify specific energetic blueprints that you want to change.

- Determine the mental, emotional, and physical origins of self-defeating behaviors and thoughts by noticing who in your family had the same patterns.

- Become aware of the areas in your life in which you are moving away from the old ways of being and acting but have not quite achieved a higher vibration. Congratulate yourself on your efforts.

- Get regular Rolfing sessions or weekly massage therapy to reprogram your physical patterns.

- Fake it until you make it.

If You Are a **Journeyman** . . .

- Enroll in a pattern-shattering workshop such as the eight-day Hoffman Process (800-506-5253) to intentionally address and eliminate worn-out habits.

- Search out role models in the areas of life in which you seek change or improvement. If you want love, find someone who exemplifies the kind of compassion and caring you admire, and learn from him or her. If you desire more money, locate a professional who is living your dream.

- Enlist the help of a mentor or guide to reinforce new modes of behavior.

- Invoke the archangel Gabriel to assist you in transforming your mental, emotional, and physical programming.

If You Are on Your Way to **Mastering** this Lesson . . .

- View every painful experience in your life as your personal participation in healing world suffering.

- For all those personal tribulations that resist transformation, pray for others in the Universe to send their healing and understanding of this lesson to you.

- Actively practice your new pattern to make it *permanent*.

- Speak of your desired habits as though they are already in place today.

Your Soul's Lesson
Shatter the Past

Your Soul's Purpose
To Pattern Your Life with Joy

Waste No Time

Use your time wisely, for it is the only thing of real value you possess on the earthly plane. When you waste it, it is a grave setback to your soul evolution. You can never be sure how many hours you have to spend in this body, your compressed psychic incubator. Your days are a gift, so use them correctly.

Be organized about how you use your time. Concentrate (which means to intensify) on things that align with your heart's desire. After all, the moment you pass worrying, getting upset, dwelling on resentments and negativity, and engaging in activities you do not believe in cannot be recouped. The soul is immortal, but it incarnates in a physical body for a designated period in order to grow, evolve, and fulfill its purpose. If you squander this life—and you certainly can choose to do so—you simply prolong your pain and suffering and hold yourself and others back from self-realization. Recognize how you misuse your days, your most precious earthly quality, *before* you arrive at death's door, for then it will be too late.

My client Emma had this realization. She was a 53-year-old wife and mother living Omaha when she was diagnosed with stage IV breast cancer, which had spread to her lymph nodes.

Overwhelmed and inconsolable about her prospects, she told me, "Sonia, it's not so much the fact that I'm dying that leaves me distraught. It's that I've never really lived my life. I've been the model wife; attended business luncheons; run the PTA; and excelled as the ideal soccer mom, block-party representative, and school fund-raiser—not because

I wanted to, but because I was afraid to say no and wanted everybody's approval.

"What I really longed for was to paint, wear red shoes, and visit Rome. And now I can't even go to the bathroom. I've thrown away my time here and can't bear to leave this earth in vain."

Emma broke my heart. She came to her self-discovery too late.

"How do I die in peace, Sonia?" she pleaded. "How can I possibly do so knowing that I wasted my life?"

It was a good question, and I reflected seriously on it. Then the answer came. "Let everyone know the truth," I answered. "Tell people not to make your mistake. Encourage them to live in their spirit rather than submit to their fears and let their dreams pass them by."

She calmed down and became quiet. "You're right," she stated. "At least that will be one honest choice I make before I pass on."

I received a copy of Emma's obituary three months later; she'd passed away about four weeks after we spoke. Her oldest daughter, a college student, sent it to me with a note saying that her mother had asked her to do so, along with the message that she'd died in peace.

My experience with Emma was a gift—a clear reminder to examine how I used my own time. In doing so, I noticed areas of colossal waste. I complained about conflicts with people, some of which had occurred years earlier; argued with my family out of boredom or a lack of proper self-care; lashed out to unload my psychic stress; and watched too much TV instead of getting the sleep I needed. The list went on and on.

I think of Emma a lot. Although she felt that her life had been pointless, she actually has helped me save lots of time, and I'm completely grateful for that. She served in her death.

Do not waste other people's time either. It is emotionally indulgent and disrespectful to break agreements, send mixed messages, arrive late for appointments (or miss them altogether), or be unaccountable. Your hours here on Earth are the only true gold you have, and while wasting your own resources is bad enough, taking away someone else's is the height of selfishness.

I know these are strong words, but they're true. Frittering away another's time, especially on self-pity and craziness, creates some of the deepest soul resentments I've encountered. I've had countless clients show up in my office, beside themselves with anger and upset over having had their time consumed in fruitless relationships.

One woman in particular, Soledad, was so distraught that she was nearly having emotional convulsions. The mother of six adults, she had one son, a creative young man named Jose, who refused to grow up and be a responsible person. She'd supported him throughout his 20s and 30s, sent him to college, paid his school and car loans, and taken in his friends and helped them as well—all under the delusion that Jose would one day assume responsibility for himself and become a self-employed designer, something he assured her would happen soon.

Instead of being serious and responsible, however, he partied, did drugs, and went out to bars night after night. He got away with his manipulations because he was a likeable person and Soledad wanted to believe in him. This ended abruptly one Christmas Eve when he drank too much with his friends and got into a car to go dancing. Jose lost control of the vehicle and hit a tree, and he and two of his passengers were killed instantly. He left over $56,000 in unpaid bills and a lot of sorrow.

All Soledad could say was, "What a waste." She'd devoted 40 years of her life to someone who wasn't committed to himself. It was a painful lesson and a terrible loss for all of them.

Soul Lesson #22 reared its painful head, and she now had only one real choice: not to use up any more time giving too much to others while neglecting her own life. I don't know what she chose to do, however, for she never came back to see me again.

In your relationships, be on time and mindful of your intentions, while respecting the needs and desires of other people. Value their priorities as your own. Although imposing your perspectives and will on others may appear to get you what you want, it will not work in the long run.

One very loving fellow, Charles, met a younger woman named Claire and immediately decided that he was supposed to be in her life to take care of her. Because she seemed lost, Charles convinced her to marry him, mother his children, and follow his instructions. In exchange, he provided her with comfort and security. Being passive and easily manipulated, Claire went along with the plan, especially seduced by the offer of ease and contentment—at least for the time being.

Claire became Charles's wife, created a lovely home, and had two sons. But she also rebelled, found a secret lover in a neighbor's husband, and ultimately left the marriage and the kids when she ran away with the new guy.

Charles was devastated. "We had an agreement," he told me. "She broke our contract."

I felt compassion for him, as he was clearly heartbroken, but I had to challenge him about their "deal."

"You say you had an agreement," I said, "but I remember it slightly differently. I recall that you hounded her relentlessly to marry you, enticing her with promises of money and safety. She submitted to your ideas, but I wouldn't exactly call that a true contract, which consists of two people fully and freely having a meeting of the minds. Your union didn't quite occur that way."

Charles had to agree. "I know I talked her into what I wanted. What a waste of time that was," he admitted.

"Yes and no," I clarified. "It was a loss in that you didn't succeed in perpetuating your agenda, but in starting over, you can use what you've learned from the experience."

You have all the time you need to accomplish anything true and meaningful that you desire, but you do not have a moment to waste. This does not mean that every moment has to be about creating high-octane results. Sometimes the most effective thing you can do is nothing.

Using your days properly means recognizing the power of rest, patience, and waiting for the natural course of events to unfold. Realize that you are not the only one acting in the Universe. The Lord of Creation is also working, and occasionally you must hold on for Divine direction.

Many years ago I had a client named Al who wanted nothing more than to be a television newscaster. His only problem was that he had a secret: He was gay and certain that his sexual orientation would doom his professional goals. Naturally, this created great frustration and fear in him, and he spent a lot of time building up what he considered an acceptable facade in order to reach his dream. To further his ruse, he dated and married a naïve young woman from Poland who didn't speak English.

He talked his way into a local, early-morning newscast position This lasted for two years, until one night, while at a gay bar, he ran into several co-workers who were amused to find him there. It was all over the office the next day. Humiliated at his cover being blown, he quit. Having no more need for a proxy wife, he also divorced. He was convinced that his career was over, so, he abandoned his hopes. That's when I met him.

My insights showed that he was simply ahead of his time and forcing the issue. I told him to be patient. "The day will come," I said, "when your sexual orientation will make absolutely no difference, and, in fact, could help you in your work."

He scoffed, "By then, I'll be facing another, even more insurmountable taboo: I'll be too old."

"Not true," I responded. "Just wait and see. In the meantime, clear up the mess you've created and get right with yourself and those whose time you've wasted."

I didn't meet with him again after that, but a few weeks ago I noticed that he's hosting a gay-oriented cable talk show. He looked supremely happy and was quite at ease. All it took was waiting for the world to catch up with him.

Using your time correctly is the final frontier in the soul's evolution. You cannot control it; you can only manage it, and ideally you should do so with great care. Spend your days on what matters, and do not devote any energy to what does not.

The root of this lesson is to be fully self-reliant. It is important and good to seek support, but not to ask, wish, or dream that anyone will carry you. Your soul seeks self-realization because that is its highest purpose. Desiring or allowing yourself to be propped up by another is a great waste of time because the spirit will rebel. You may not know when, but you can be certain that it will.

To see how you use your time, wear a watch that has an alarm and set it to ring once an hour for a week (except when you're sleeping). When it goes off, note whether you're spending the moment wisely or wasting it.

We are creatures of habit. I've noticed that what you do in a week is relatively indicative of how you pass your months, and even years. Be aware of your focus, conversations, and emotional and mental states. How many hours are you squandering? This experiment will be quite revealing.

When you embrace time as gold to expend carefully on what is important and true for you, life becomes eternal. You stretch your minutes and no longer chase them, and they serve you and your growth. The more you value them, the more you will have. Ultimately you will transcend the clock altogether and turn your existence into an exquisite work of self-realization. Greatness *can* be achieved in the span of one incarnation, when you use it wisely. Just look at Leonardo da Vinci or Michelangelo, to cite a couple of examples of what is possible.

Treat time as the precious commodity that it is, and dole it out only on worthy endeavors. Doing this will take you directly toward mastery of purpose on a soul level and will put you fully in charge of your life.

Now you can apply this lesson.

— If you waste vast amounts of time watching TV, talking on the phone, complaining about others, or fretting about the future, or are careless and late to appointments or miss them altogether . . . then you are a **student** in learning this lesson.

— If you attempt to get organized even though you are not always successful; let phone calls go to voice mail when you are involved in a project or more important things; feel rushed, pressured, overwhelmed, and overbooked; do not get adequate sleep; or do not have enough time for what and whom you love . . . then you are an **apprentice.**

— If you are fair in your agreements, respectful and prompt in your commitments, and clear and direct in your intentions; listen closely; or value and take time for what you cherish most . . . then you are a **journeyman.**

— If you are guarded and highly selective about how you spend your hours; do not waste a second dwelling on the past, instead quickly clearing up what needs attention so that you can live in the now; maintain a comfortable pace and find moments for the unexpected; value the important people in your life more than anything and make it your intention to share positive quality time with them; or are grateful for every day you have . . . then you are on your way to **mastering** this lesson.

If You Are a **Student** . . .

- Get a day planner and write down your goals and commitments.

- Schedule in appointments to renew and regenerate yourself.

- Allow 15 extra minutes to get to every meeting or visit.

- Turn off the TV and make the decision to serve others.

If You Are an **Apprentice** . . .

- Give yourself some time to reflect before agreeing to commitments.

- Focus on your priorities and intentions and clearly communicate them to others in a timely fashion.

- Listen closely to people to discern their plans and desires.

- First take care of yourself before moving on to help others during your day.

If You Are a **Journeyman** . . .

- Take 15 minutes for yourself before you begin your day.

- Never waste time on old business. Do what you need to in order to finish it. If it comes up in conversation, quietly but firmly change the subject and move on.

- Allow a maximum of five minutes for an argument or squabble. After that, take a break and come back when you are less emotional and more clear about what you want.

- Practice breathing, calming, and centering yourself before responding to difficulties. Notice that *reaction* is a waste of time, while *response* is productive.

- Turn off the TV, computer, and iPod, and enjoy the present.

If You Are on Your Way to **Mastering** this Lesson . . .

- Allocate daily moments to be grateful and enjoy the now.

- Make no commitment that you do not intend to honor fully.

- Take time every day for important relationships and activities without apologizing for doing so.

- Say no without hesitation to things that waste your time.

- Fully accept all experiences as your soul's creation, and use your life to embrace the lessons you are here to learn rather than fighting and struggling against them.

- Above all, make it a priority to enjoy yourself every day.

Your Soul's Lesson
Use Your Time Wisely

Your Soul's Purpose
Become the Timely Master of Your Life

Epilogue

And so, dear ones, our tutorial for reclaiming your Divine heritage draws to a close. We are grateful to have had your attention throughout these pages and lovingly assure you that we—along with all the Light Beings in the Universe in service to our Great Creator—are ever present to continue guiding and supporting your soul's learning and growth in every possible way.

The information conveyed in this curriculum may at times appear difficult and overwhelming to assimilate and implement, yet we assure you that it is not new to you. Your spirit's plan and purpose was agreed upon before your present incarnation and is inscribed in every cell of your body. Our directive from the Lord of Life is to reactivate what is lying dormant in your consciousness and awaken your Higher Self's commitment to your true nature. If you learn these lessons, they will lead you to fulfill your greatest potential. If you choose to call forth your inner essence, you will achieve understanding naturally and with grace.

As we conclude our time together, we leave you with one final directive that best summarizes and simplifies all we have previously laid out: that is, to always live with an open heart; compassionate acceptance; and unconditional, forgiving love for yourself and all of the Universe's creatures and creations. This decision will clear the way for mastering your soul lessons with ease and guide you to joyfully meet your spirit's highest purpose, which is to glorify God and serve as an ambassador of Light on Earth.

As always, you rest forever in the heart, mind, and spirit of the Lord of the Universe. Breathe in, accept, and live your Divinity; and cherish the gift of your life.

In the deepest gratitude and service, we withdraw in love and await your further contact. To call upon us and all the Light Beings available to you, simply be receptive and ask for help. We hear you and will readily respond.

— With blessings and great love,
Joachim and the Emissaries of the Third Ray

Writing this book was quite an experience. I actually feel sad that the Emissaries have finished their instruction and are stepping back now. I came to look forward to every writing session, feeling like a student showing up for class, eager to learn—and boy, did I!

Being so intimately connected with their sacred vibration over the course of the six months that it took to create this book has greatly affected and changed me. My heart has softened and opened wider than before. I felt wave upon wave of intense compassion for myself and all of humanity as I wrote, and this journey increased my ability to care even more. I was moved to become less self-centered as I began to realize on the deepest level just how truly connected we are to one another. My tendency to love selectively has also largely subsided because I now feel that my fellow souls are truly part of me.

When I look around at the sea of humanity, I like what I see—even with our craziness. We're so foolish at times as we struggle to find ourselves—especially at the present moment as the world conveys horrifying images to us via the television and newspapers—but we're still all lovable and need to believe that, in spite of what we do.

I also began to recognize how stubbornly judgmental my ego can be, and am consciously working to tame her. At least I can laugh when she rears her insecure head these days, knowing that this isn't me or my spirit acting up and causing me stress. Consequently, my days are lighter and easier, and my frustration and upset have decreased considerably.

My attention is more centered on the present as well. With the help of Joachim and the Emissaries, I rarely think about tomorrow or the past anymore. I now clearly understand on the deepest level that Earth is soul school and that the Higher Self is eternal. Once a day has passed, that lesson is over and it's time to move on to the next. Dwelling on what is gone is the greatest waste of our precious gift of life and serves no useful purpose whatsoever.

The best part of working with the Emissaries on this book is that everything I've been learning and teaching over the course of my life has settled into me even more profoundly. Nothing on these pages is necessarily new; I'd already been introduced to almost all of these concepts at some point. It's just that this time, I was able to hear the wisdom in a whole new way—I felt it in my bones.

As a race, we must move into a higher vibration in order to continue to live together on this planet. We can't keep progressing at the slow pace we've maintained. We must act in a more loving way, beginning with ourselves. We need to start now if we hope to survive and thrive as a group consciousness. I'm grateful for this expanding awareness.

When the Emissaries brought this volume to a close, I asked them, "What's next?"

I heard in response, "Have compassionate acceptance and unconditional love and forgiveness every moment of your life. There is nothing more profound, greater, or more urgent than this."

I join you in taking this information into my being and absorbing it. My spirit says let's work together, help each other, and continue to be open to receiving the generous support of the heavens. It's the only way to secure a healthy future. I'm willing and I hope you are, too.

I send you all my love,
Sonia

Λcknowledgments

I'd like to thank my mother and father, Sonia and Paul Choquette, for giving me a spirited life. To my husband, for being a great five-sensory support person and trusting me and the world of soul through all its wild turns. To my daughters, Sonia and Sabrina, whom I love so much, thank you for being my sparkle, laughter, and joy. To Lu Ann Glatzmaier and Joan Smith, my soul sisters, for helping prepare me to receive such profound and loving guidance. To my spirit teachers Dr. Tully and Charlie Goodman for overseeing my purpose in life.

And to my newest spirit helpers, Louise Hay, Reid Tracy, and the entire Hay House staff, for your belief in me and your tireless support. To Julia Cameron, my dear and most beloved friend and writing champion, without whose help I would never have become an author. To my editors, Bruce Clorfene and Linda Kahn, for helping me shape my first channeled book and enjoying the subject along the way. To Ryan Kaiser and Anne Kaiser, for helping me get my work into the world and listening to my complaints and worries throughout the entire process. To Nancy Levin and her magical elves, for seamlessly guiding my flight onto the public stage. Most of all, to God, for blessing me again and again in allowing me to share these messages with the world.

About the Author

Sonia Choquette is a world-renowned author, storyteller, vibrational healer, and six-sensory spiritual teacher in international demand for her guidance, wisdom, and capacity to heal the soul. She's the author of eight best-selling books, including *Diary of a Psychic* and *Trust Your Vibes;* and numerous audio programs and card decks. Sonia was educated at the University of Denver and the Sorbonne in Paris, and holds a Ph.D. in metaphysics from the American Institute of Holistic Theology. She resides with her family in Chicago.

Website: **www.soniachoquette.com**

Hay House Titles of Related Interest

*THE DIVINE MATRIX: Bridging Time, Space, Miracles,
and Belief,* by Gregg Braden

*FOUR ACTS OF PERSONAL POWER: How to Heal Your Past
and Create a Positive Future,* by Denise Linn

*THE POWER OF INFINITE LOVE & GRATITUDE:
An Evolutionary Journey to Awakening Your Spirit,*
by Dr. Darren R. Weissman

POWER OF THE SOUL: Inside Wisdom for an Outside World,
by John Holland

*REMEMBERING THE FUTURE: The Path to Recovering
Intuition,* by Colette Baron-Reid

*SPIRITUAL CONNECTIONS: How to Find Spirituality
Throughout All the Relationships in Your Life,* by Sylvia Browne

*THE TIMES OF OUR LIVES: Extraordinary True Stories
of Synchronicity, Destiny, Meaning, and Purpose,*
by Louise L. Hay & Friends; compiled & edited by Jill Kramer

*YOUR IMMORTAL REALITY: How to Break
the Cycle of Birth and Death,* by Gary R. Renard

All of the above are available at your local bookstore,
or may be ordered by contacting Hay House (see last page).

We hope you enjoyed this Hay House book.
If you'd like to receive a free catalog featuring
additional Hay House books and products, or if you'd
like information about the Hay Foundation, please contact:

Hay House, Inc.
P.O. Box 5100
Carlsbad, CA 92018-5100

(760) 431-7695 or (800) 654-5126
(760) 431-6948 (fax) or (800) 650-5115 (fax)
www.hayhouse.com® • www.hayfoundation.org

Published and distributed in Australia by: Hay House Australia Pty. Ltd.,
18/36 Ralph St., Alexandria NSW 2015 • *Phone:* 612-9669-4299
Fax: 612-9669-4144 • www.hayhouse.com.au

Published and distributed in the United Kingdom by: Hay House UK, Ltd.,
292B Kensal Rd., London W10 5BE • *Phone:* 44-20-8962-1230
Fax: 44-20-8962-1239 • www.hayhouse.co.uk

Published and distributed in the Republic of South Africa by:
Hay House SA (Pty), Ltd., P.O. Box 990, Witkoppen 2068
Phone/Fax: 27-11-706-6612 • orders@psdprom.co.za

Published in India by: Hay House Publishers India, Muskaan Complex,
Plot No. 3, B-2, Vasant Kunj, New Delhi 110 070 • *Phone:* 91-11-4176-1620
Fax: 91-11-4176-1630 • www.hayhouseindia.co.in

Distributed in Canada by: Raincoast , 9050 Shaughnessy St.,
Vancouver, B.C. V6P 6E5 • *Phone:* (604) 323-7100
Fax: (604) 323-2600 • www.raincoast.com

Tune in to **HayHouseRadio.com**® for the best in inspirational
talk radio featuring top Hay House authors! And, sign up via the
Hay House USA Website to receive the Hay House online newsletter
and stay informed about what's going on with your favorite authors.
You'll receive bimonthly announcements about Discounts and Offers,
Special Events, Product Highlights, Free Excerpts, Giveaways, and more!
www.hayhouse.com®